BEADS & BRAIDS

Jacqui Carey

Published by CAREY COMPANY

Acknowledgements

The name on the cover is, in so many ways, irrelevant.
As usual this has been a team effort involving family and friends.
Patience, encouragement, advice and support have been supplied
by so many. Moreover, the practicalities of this book would not
have been possible without the following:
Diana East, Joan Howes, my parents, my children, Richard and
Madilyn and last but definitely not least my husband, Paul.

Although all the designs in this book are original, they have been
made possible by all that has been done before them.
Therefore, this book is dedicated to the many who have worked,
often without recognition, to add to the wealth of knowledge and
inspiration that surrounds us.

Colour reproduction, design and photography by Carey Company.
Printed by the Devonshire Press Ltd, Torquay, UK.
Published by: Carey Company

ISBN 0-9523225-2-8

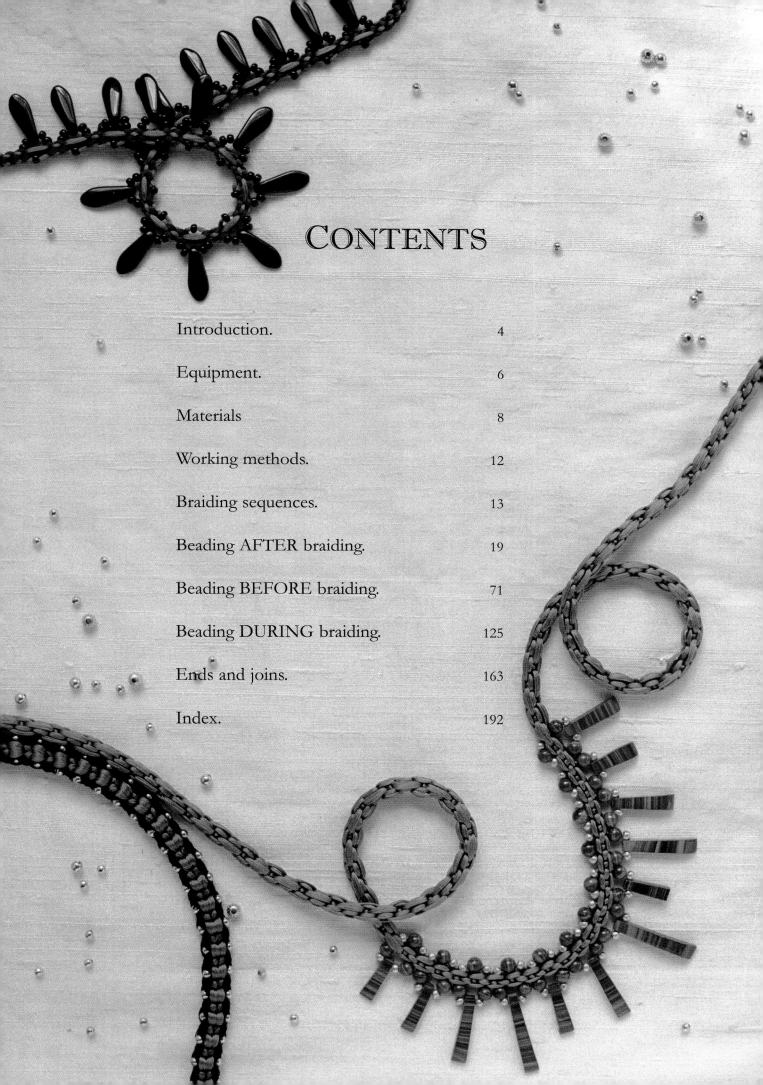

CONTENTS

INTRODUCTION

Decoration is a passion that is both universal and historical. It can serve a functional purpose or be purely frivolous. Beads and braids are no exception. Both beads and braids can trace their origins to the dawn of civilisation and the combination of the two subjects is nothing new. As beads and braids complement each other so well, it is not surprising that examples can be found in most cultures (illustrated by the two photographs on this page). However, with such a choice of materials and styles within each technique there are endless possibilities. This means that although this subject has been covered before there is still plenty of scope for new ideas.

Braids can be made in a whole host of different ways. This book concentrates on the Japanese art of Kumihimo made on a Marudai. This round stand is an elegant and adaptable piece of equipment. It provides the braider with maximum control. Consequently beads can be added with more ease and versatility than with other methods. Nevertheless, many of the examples shown in this book can be reproduced using other braiding techniques (see photograph opposite).

Forty different methods of combining beads and braids are explored, divided into four chapters:

1. Beads added after the braids have been completed.
2. Beads added to the threads before braiding begins.
3. Beads added during the braiding process.
4. Beaded ends and joins.

Each of these forty methods is illustrated with three different samples. Every sample can be reproduced by following the detailed instructions and diagrams.

As the book focuses on the combination of beads and braids, it is not intended as an introduction to Kumihimo. This information can be found in other books such as 'The Beginners Guide to Braiding' (details on inside back cover). It is advisable to cover this ground first so that concentration can be placed on the new ideas found within this book.

Beaded braids made using different techniques.
From left to right: Slotted board, French knitting and Macrame.

Having said that, readers do not have to be expert braidmakers to use this book to recreate stunning results. The braids used in the samples have deliberately been kept simple; just eight bobbins are required and only nine different sequences of moves are used. This offers a good range of braid structures whilst maintaining an easy to follow format. An effort has also been made to use beads that are readily available whilst exploring a broad range of different bead types.

The samples are intended to illustrate each method. Once the ideas are understood, they can be used with a multitude of other braid structures and bead types.

There are so many variations awaiting exploration, an infinite number of possibilities: too many for one book or one person. With such a wealth of opportunity it is hoped that this book will act as a springboard, providing the technical ideas for everyone to experience the thrill of creativity.

To this end the gallery selection in each chapter of the book is intended as inspiration and encouragement for personal exploration.

Opposite page: *Detail of a purse from Afghanistan, trimmed with a beaded braid.*
Bracelet of Chinese knots and Amber beads.

EQUIPMENT

The braiding technique used in this book is based on traditional Kumihimo made on a Marudai (round stand) using bobbins, counterbalance weights, weightbag, S-hook and chopstick. This can be traditional wooden equipment or the lower cost acrylic version. It is also possible to use a 'home-made' apparatus such as can be seen here.

The round, top surface of the Marudai, known as the mirror, needs to be kept smooth. A soft, leather cover can be made to protect the mirror if you are concerned about the beads marking the surface (especially applicable for the 'beading before braiding' chapter).

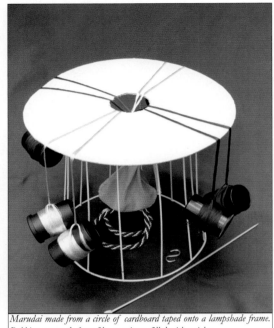

Marudai made from a circle of cardboard taped onto a lampshade frame. Bobbins are made from film cannisters filled with weights.

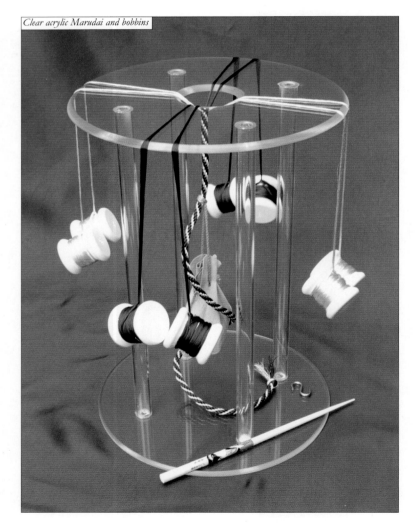

Clear acrylic Marudai and bobbins

All the samples are made with just eight bobbins, although sometimes different weight bobbins are used. It is possible to reproduce the samples using different bobbins to those specified in the instructions; though do be sure to alter the counterbalance weight accordingly. Other sundry items required for braiding include scissors, warping posts, tape measure, needles and cotton thread (for tying warps).

Several items that are useful for the beadwork include beading needle, beading thread, a small crochet hook and pliers.

*Traditional wooden Marudai and bobbins together
with assorted braids and ropes of thread.*

MATERIALS

THREAD

A warp is the collection of threads used to produce a braid. Threads can be of any thread type. In fact any material that can be manipulated can be braided, even hair, wire, paper, clay etc. This gives rise to an enormous range of possible outcomes. However, silk is the traditional material used for Kumihimo. For consistency all the samples in this book use Japanese silk or Biron (synthetic silk). These threads make up into lustrous braids with crisp, well-defined stitches.

Thread size can be measured by comparing length and weight. The international Tex count gives the weight in grams of 1000m of that thread with the number after the dash representing the ply. The Japanese silk is a three-ply continuous fibre with a Tex count of 22/3. The Biron is a marginally thicker thread with a Tex count of 26/3. These threads are normally supplied in pre-made 'ropes', a rope being a quantity of threads lightly twisted together.

This is a standard measure comprising 42 strands of silk measuring 2.7metres(9ft) in length. A Biron rope is the same length and thickness, but comprises only 39 strands.

These ropes are typically used to make obi-jime, the Kumihimo belt around the kimono. The standard procedure is to work with one rope on each bobbin. However, alternative divisions can be made. For example, a half-length rope (1.35m) on each bobbin still produces a suitable amount of finished braid.

Divisions of thickness are less convenient and can be approached in two ways. Simple splits, such as halving the thickness (giving approximately 20 strands for each bobbin) are best done with the rope on the Marudai. This is illustated in the following example. Here a warp is prepared for Sample 1A (page 21). Make a warp of four ropes, (one green, one purple and two blue). These need to be halved to provide the thread for eight bobbins.

Smooth out one rope so that all the threads are lying parallel (Fig. 1). Then starting at the top of the rope, nearest the tie, divide the threads in to two equal groups (Fig. 2). Gradually ease the threads apart, working down to the end of the rope. Then attach a bobbin on to each group of threads. Repeat this procedure for each rope.

When fewer strands are required, it is easier to use a different approach. Work from the centre of a rope and smooth out the threads until they are parallel. Take just one strand and pull it away from the rope (Fig. 3). Repeat this process until you have the required number of strands. An option is to wrap a small piece of paper around the rope to help keep the remaining threads in an orderly group.

For the samples in this book you can make warps using different threads to those specified. To match the conditions of each sample, the Tex number can be used to calculate an alternative. However, a simple guess can also be tried although any changes can alter the appearance of the finished piece.

Fig. 1

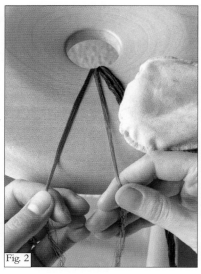
Fig. 2

Fig. 3

BEADS

Beads come in a huge variety of shapes and sizes. The materials they are made of are equally as numerous, from ancient bone, stone and shell, through glass and clay to modern acrylics and polymers. With such diversity of beads, the possibilities are endless. Even everyday items such as pasta, paperclips, keys and plastic toys can be converted into beads. These can be used to add a unique and personal touch to the finished result.

However, the samples described in this book utilise beads that are readily available.

ROCAILLE/SEED

These small, glass beads are available in a range of sizes (10's, 8's etc). The larger the number, the smaller the bead. However, the sizes do vary considerably between different sources. Even beads from the same source have a tendency to vary in both bead size and hole size, which can be frustrating in certain circumstances. However, the subtle irregularities of these beads tend to give character and life to projects. The beads are usually shaped in a slightly squashed sphere.

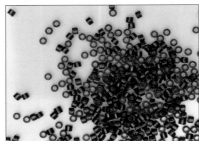

DELICA

These are also small glass beads but they are of a uniform cylindrical shape. The holes are also regular in size. The wall of each bead is quite thin giving a large hole size in comparison to the bead size.

BUGLES

These are long, glass beads with a cross-section of a circle or a hexagon. Their width and length vary depending on the source, as do their hole sizes.

FACET

Faceted beads are many sided. Although facets are usually associated with gemstones, faceted glass beads are readily available. The refraction of light on their cut surfaces gives a better result than the plastic substitutes.

PENDANT

Pendants are available in many different materials. Their unifying feature is that the bead hole is placed at the top of the bead. This hole can be bored sideways through the bead or through the face. Another option is for a top pin to create a hole above the bead, as can be seen here.

STRING
This term refers to many beads strung together on a beading thread. These beads can be of any type and are usually threaded on to a special, strong thread.

PLASTIC SHAPE
Nowadays, there are many types of plastic beads. They come in a range of different shapes and finishes such as the gold coloured rosettes illustrated.

PONY
These are similar to rocaille beads except they are much larger (Approximately 8mm in diameter).Originally made with glass, they are now also available in plastic.

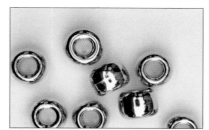

DROPS
These are small teardrop shaped beads. They hang like little pendants because the holes are at the top (thin end) of the bead.

POLYMER CLAY
These beads are made from synthetic clay as opposed to natural clay. The polymer is easier to work than natural clay. It is also easier to set hard.

CLOISONNE
These are a particular style of enamelled bead. The different coloured patterns are separated with thin metal strips.

LAMPWORK
This particular technique produces beads that are hand made by shaping glass over a gas flame.

There are forty different methods shown in this book. The techniques progress with ideas often evolving in sequence. Each method is numbered and illustrated with three samples A, B and C. Sample A is usually the easiest of the three. The specific details of each sample are given and can therefore be reproduced. Each sample has a table of Braid and Bead details as illustrated below. This gives all the details required for the sample.

Braiding sequence

This refers to the type of braid used to make the sample. The sequence of moves required to produce each braid can be found on pages 13 to 17.

Bobbin weight

This is the weight of each bobbin used to produce the braid.

Weight bag

This gives the amount of counterbalance weight placed in the weightbag.

Finished length

This gives an approximate size of the finished sample (not including the tassels).

Circle diagram.

The large circle represents the Marudai surface viewed from above. The smaller circles show the starting positions of each bobbin wound with different colours. It is these starting positions that dictate the surface pattern of the braid.

Warp details.

This refers to the threads used to make the braid. Each circle represents a bobbin wound with the specific threads shown. For simplicity, the traditional rope (of full thickness) is referred to as containing forty strands and a half rope thickness as containing twenty strands.

Bead details

This give the quantity, name and approximate dimensions of the beads required to reproduce the sample.

Working

The text with this title gives the specific instructions required to construct the sample. References to specific positions on the mirror are given in terms of compass points. North being

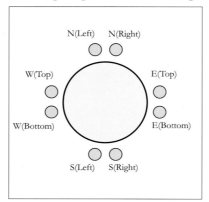

at the top of the circle indicating the position furthest from the braider.

The samples are intended as an initial guide. They are open to experimentation and you may wish to alter some of the details to suit your individual tastes. For example we all braid with subtle variations in tension and therefore the weight in the weight bag may need to be altered accordingly.

It has already been noted that beads and their hole size can vary and this may need to be taken into consideration. In some cases it may be necessary to alter the number of threads used on a bobbin to compensate for the difference in bead hole size. Similarly, if different thread types are used, changes may have to be made to the warp details.

It is hoped that once the technique is understood, the idea can be tried under different conditions; different types of thread, different braid structures, different patterns and different beads. Of course it should be noted that any changes will effect the appearance of the finished piece and this is where exciting discoveries can be made!

There are so many variations awaiting exploration, an infinite number of possibilities: too many for one book or one person. With such a wealth of opportunity it is hoped that this book will act as a springboard, providing the technical ideas for everyone to experience the thrill of creativity.

To this end the gallery selection in each section of the book is intended as inspiration and encouragement for personal exploration.

SAMPLE 3B

BRAID DETAILS:

Braiding sequence:
Bobbin weight:
Weight bag:
Finished length:

BEAD DETAILS:

WARP DETAILS:

20 strands of :
20 strands of :
20 strands of :

Just nine different braids are used to make all of the samples shown in this book. It is advisable to get familiar with the sequences of moves before attempting any beadwork. This ensures that concentration can be placed on the rest of the instructions given. It also reduces the amount of page turning required!

The sequences of moves are depicted with large circles representing the mirror viewed from above. The smaller circles represent the bobbins positioned around the edge of the Marudai. Each move of the sequence is numbered in order. The arrows show the path that the bobbins must take to reach their new positions. References to R/H and L/H refer to bobbins being lifted with the right-hand and left-hand.

The photo of the finished braid is shown in monotone to highlight the structure of the braid produced.

The point of braiding is the place at which the threads intersect to form the braid. The photograph shows the point of braiding at the end of a sequence - ready to restart with movement 1.

LADDER BRAID

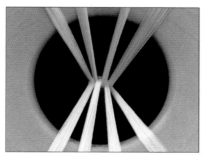

The repetition of moves 1-4 results in the production of two four-bobbin braids lying parallel to each other. Moves 5 and 6 lock these two braids together forming the 'rungs' of the ladder braid.

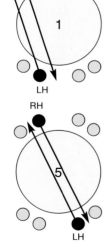

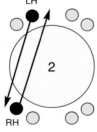

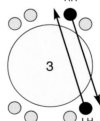

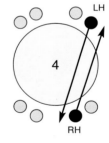

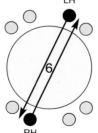

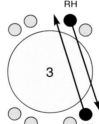

Work the following sequence of moves:

1, 2, 3, 4
1, 2, 3, 4
1, 2, 3, 4
5, 6.

ROUND BRAID ONE

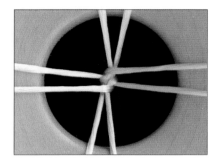

This braid is created by the continuous repetition of just two moves. The result is a firm round braid.

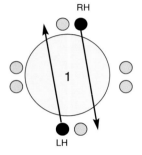

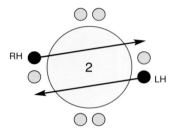

ROUND BRAID TWO

This is another braid that has a round cross-section, although this one has a more 'knobbly' textured exterior. In some cases (such as Sample 15) a variation of this braid is used. By repeating some moves more than others an interesting effect is obtained.

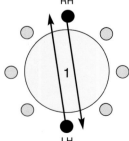

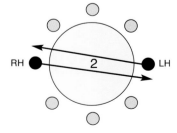

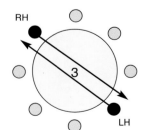

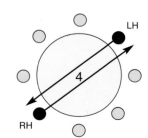

FLAT BRAID ONE

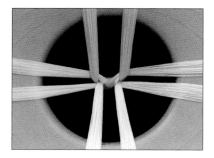

A rhythmic set of moves that produces a flat braid. Although both sides appear the same they are, in fact, different.

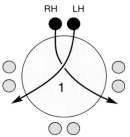
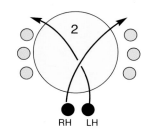
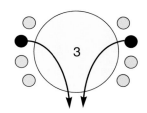
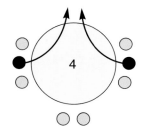

FLAT BRAID TWO

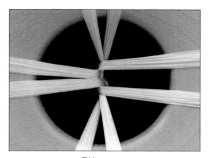

This is a more complex sequence of moves, which results in a flat braid of unusual structure. Both sides are distinctively different.

The threads get worked at different rates. The ones on the bobbins starting in positions N(left), E(top) and S(left) are used up the quickest, whilst the threads on the bobbins starting in positions E(bottom) and W(top) are used the least.

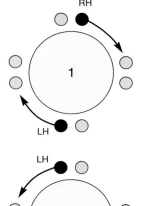
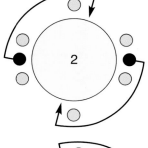
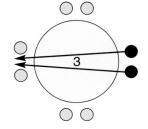
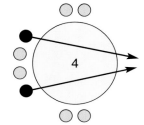
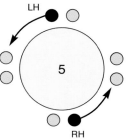
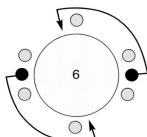
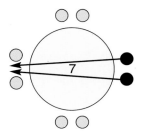
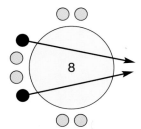

15

SPIRAL BRAID ONE

These moves produce a braid that gently spirals in a double helix structure.

The warp threads are not worked evenly for this braid. The threads on the bobbins in position N(right) and S(left) are used up quicker than all the others.

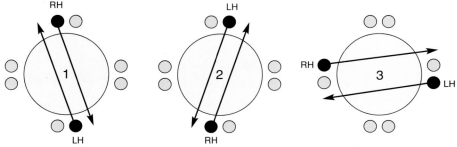

SPIRAL BRAID TWO

Another double helix spiral. However, this one is a much tighter, more exaggerated spiral than the one previously shown. It is not as stable and requires more attention to maintaining a steady tension. Particular attention should be paid to the bobbins used in movement 1. Ensure that they are always keeping the tension on their threads.

The threads on the bobbins in position N and S are used up quicker than all the others.

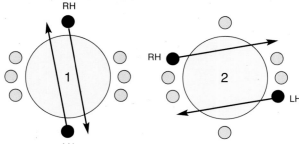

RECTANGULAR BRAID

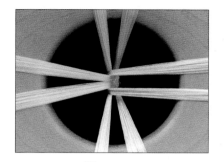

This sequence of six moves results in a rectangular braid with distinctive 'dimples' on each side.

The threads on the bobbins starting in positions E(top) and E(bottom) are used up quicker than all the others.

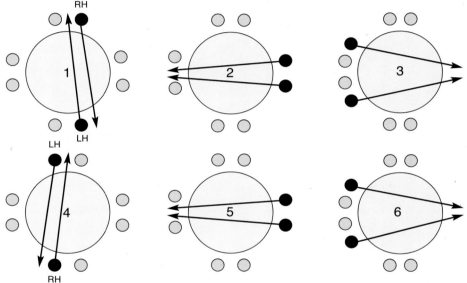

SQUARE BRAID

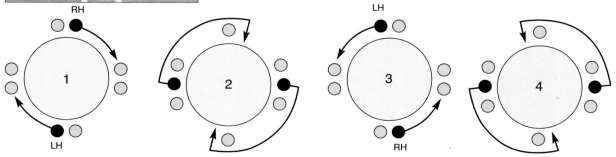

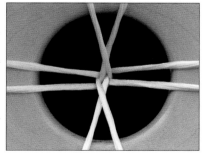

Here the moves work in rotational symmetry giving a different rhythm to the braiding. The moves can be thought of as a 'slide-jump two' action that produces a twill structured square braid.

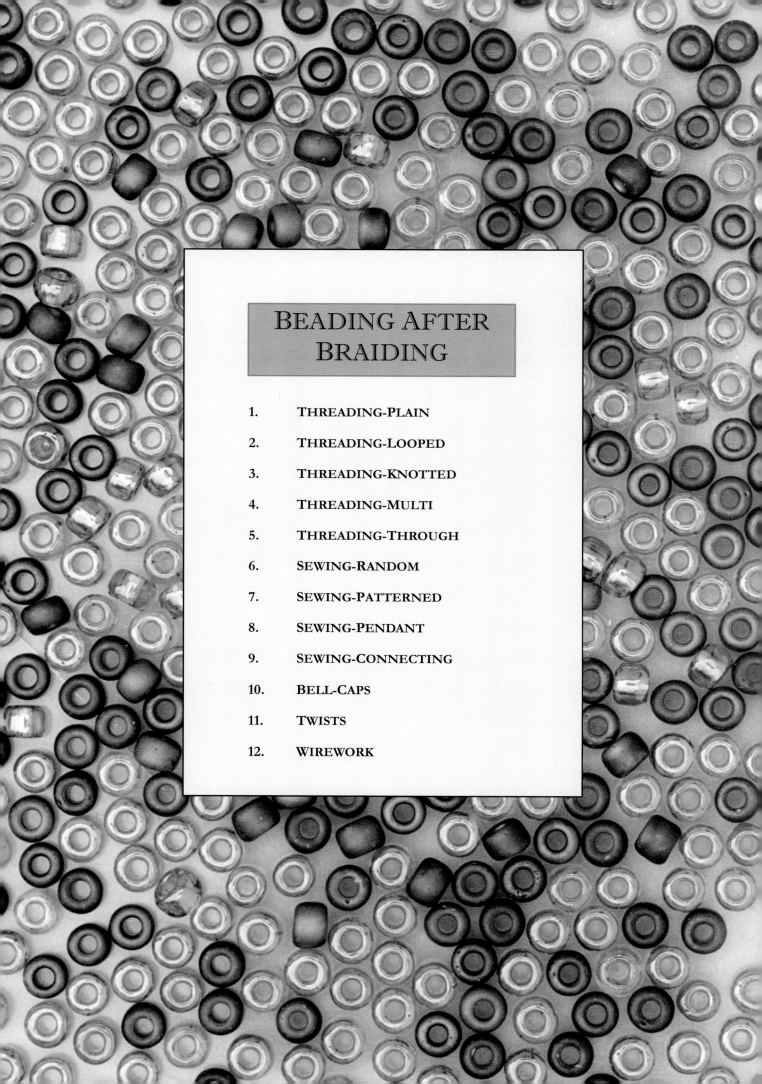

BEADING AFTER BRAIDING

1. THREADING-PLAIN

2. THREADING-LOOPED

3. THREADING-KNOTTED

4. THREADING-MULTI

5. THREADING-THROUGH

6. SEWING-RANDOM

7. SEWING-PATTERNED

8. SEWING-PENDANT

9. SEWING-CONNECTING

10. BELL-CAPS

11. TWISTS

12. WIREWORK

1 THREADING-PLAIN

This is the most obvious way of combining beads and braids. Beads are usually strung on to a thread or cord. However, handmade braids provide not just a strong foundation for the beads but can become an attractive and integral part of the finished piece. The most important factor of this method is that the finished braid must fit through the bead hole. Therefore, before braiding commences, the size of the bead hole must be compared to the total number of warp threads being used.

The following three samples produce braids that fit snugly in the bead hole. The braids are made under tension and will relax when finished, causing them to expand slightly in diameter. This is sufficient to stop the beads from slipping along the braid. A more permanent solution can be obtained by placing a small amount of glue around the braid before slipping the bead into position over it.

Alternatively smaller beads can be sewn on to the braid to keep the larger beads in place. This is illustrated in Sample 38B.

If you wish to thread beads over a tasselled end, it is worth wrapping the tassel in a roll of paper (See Fig. 1.1). This keeps all the loose threads together and prevents them from snagging on any rough points inside the bead. However, the paper will marginally add to the diameter of everything going through the bead hole so use thin paper and keep it rolled tightly.

Another option is to make a second, temporary whipping over the end of the tassel (See Fig.1.2). This will help to keep all the loose threads together as they are passed through the bead and it can be removed afterwards.

Alternatively, make a 'blunt' end by trimming down to the permanent whipping and removing all the loose tassel threads (See Fig. 1.3).

If pushing the braid through the bead is a problem, try pulling the braid through. Temporarily knot a finer thread over the braid and use this to pull the braid through the bead (See Fig. 1.4).

Fig.1.1

Fig.1.3

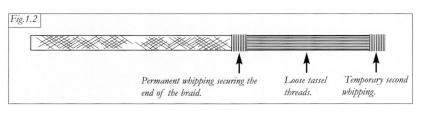

Fig.1.2

Permanent whipping securing the end of the braid.   *Loose tassel threads.*   *Temporary second whipping.*

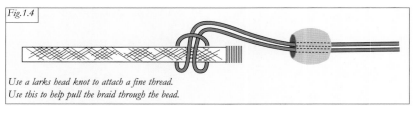

Fig.1.4

Use a larks head knot to attach a fine thread.
Use this to help pull the braid through the bead.

Detail of beads threaded onto Braid Sample 1A

1. THREADING-PLAIN

SAMPLE 1A

BRAID DETAILS:

Braiding sequence: Round Braid One

Bobbin weight: 70gms (2½oz)

Weight bag: 275gms (10oz)

Finished length: 140cm (55in)

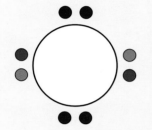

BEAD DETAILS:

20 'Melons' - gold coloured plastic
    Bead size: 10mm (¹³⁄₃₂in)   Hole size: 4mm (⁵⁄₃₂in)

WARP DETAILS:

● 20 strands of blue Biron, 2.7m (9ft) long

● 20 strands of purple Biron, 2.7m (9ft) long

● 20 strands of green Biron, 2.7m (9ft) long

WORKING

There are many ways of preparing a warp. Use any method that is familiar to you to produce a warp with the details as shown above. Use this warp to produce the round braid. Complete the braid by making a secure whipping at both ends.

The beads can now be threaded directly on to the finished braid. (Use the tips described opposite)

Sample 1A

1. THREADING-PLAIN

SAMPLE 1B

BRAID DETAILS:

Braiding sequence: Round Braid One

Bobbin weight: 70gms (2½oz)

Weight bag: 275gms (10oz)

Finished length: 70cm (27½in)

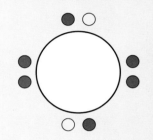

BEAD DETAILS:

2 'Spacers' - gold plated metal
  Bead size: 5mm(³⁄₁₆in) Hole size: 4mm(⁵⁄₃₂in)
2 'Melons' - gold coloured plastic
  Bead size: 10mm(¹³⁄₃₂in) Hole size: 4mm(⁵⁄₃₂in)
1 'Sphere' - gold coloured plastic
  Bead size: 16mm(⁵⁄₈in) Hole size: 4mm(⁵⁄₃₂in)

WARP DETAILS:

● 20 strands of purple Biron, 1.35m (53in) long
○ 20 strands of gold Metallic Biron, 1.35m (53in) long

WORKING

Prepare a braid using the warp details shown. Thread the beads on to the braid in the following order: spacer, melon, sphere, melon, spacer.

Sample 1B

SAMPLE 1C

BRAID DETAILS:

Braiding sequence: Round Braid One

Bobbin weight: 70gms (2½oz)

Weight bag: 275gms (10oz)

Finished length: 70cm (27½in)

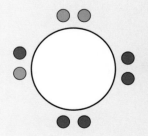

BEAD DETAILS:

2 'Spacers' - gold plated metal
  Bead size: 5mm(³⁄₁₆in) Hole size: 4mm(⁵⁄₃₂in)
2 'Melons' - gold coloured plastic
  Bead size: 10mm(¹³⁄₃₂in) Hole size: 4mm(⁵⁄₃₂in)
1 'Sphere' - gold coloured plastic
  Bead size: 16mm(⁵⁄₈in) Hole size: 4mm(⁵⁄₃₂in)

WARP DETAILS:

● 20 strands of purple Biron, 1.35m (53in) long
● 20 strands of green Biron, 1.35m (53in) long

WORKING

Prepare a braid using the warp details shown. Thread the beads on to the braid in the following order: spacer, melon, sphere, melon, spacer.

Sample 1C

2 THREADING -LOOPED

Threading a braid back through the bead creates a loop. This means that consideration must be given to the braid size to ensure that it will fit twice through the chosen bead.

Looped threading can be used to display beads to great effect. It is particularly useful for changing the orientation of a bead, as seen in the following diagrams.

Vertical.

Take the braid through the larger bead. Then thread the braid through a smaller bead before taking it back through the hole of the larger bead. The small bead acts as a stopper preventing the loop of braid from disappearing back through the larger bead. This way of threading allows the large bead to hang vertically (See Fig. 2.1).

Horizontal.

Alternatively, take the braid through the small bead first. Then thread the braid through the large bead and back through the small one. Now the large bead hangs horizontally with the small bead drawing the loop of braid together (See Fig. 2.2).

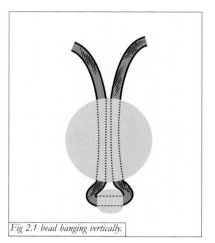

Fig 2.1 bead hanging vertically.

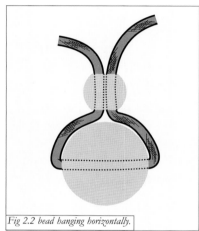

Fig 2.2 bead hanging horizontally.

Detail of Sample 2B.

Detail of Sample 2C.

23

2. THREADING-LOOPED

SAMPLE 2A

BRAID DETAILS:

Braiding sequence: Spiral Braid One

Bobbin weight: 70gms (2½oz)

Weight bag: 275gms (10oz)

Finished length: 80cm (31½in)

BEAD DETAILS:

1 'Spacer' - gold plated metal
Bead size: 6x4mm(¼x ⁵⁄₃₂in) Hole size: 4mm(⁵⁄₃₂in)

1 ' Clear' - acrylic
Bead size: 18mm(²³⁄₃₂in) Hole size: 5mm(³⁄₁₆in)

WARP DETAILS:

- 10 strands of ochre silk, 1.35m (53in) long
- 20 strands of cream silk, 1.35m (53in) long

WORKING

Prepare a braid using the above details. Thread the finished braid through the beads so that the large bead is hanging vertically (see instructions on page 23).

Don't forget the tips on threading braids through beads can be found on page 20.

SAMPLE 2A

SAMPLE 2B

SAMPLE 2C

SAMPLE 2B

BEAD DETAILS:

1 'Spacer' - gold plated metal
    Bead size: 6x4mm(¼.⁵⁄₃₂in) Hole size: 4mm(⁵⁄₃₂in)
1 'Large' - painted ceramic
    Bead size: 25mm(1in) Hole size: 5mm(³⁄₁₆in)

BRAID DETAILS:

Braiding sequence: Spiral Braid One
Bobbin weight: 70gms (2½oz)
Weight bag: 275gms (10oz.
Finished length: 80cm (31½in)

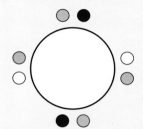

WARP DETAILS:

○ 16 strands of cream silk, 1.35m (53in) long
◒ 16 strands of ochre silk, 1.35m (53in) long
◒ 8 strands of blue silk, 1.35m (53in) long
● 8 strands of navy silk, 1.35m (53in) long

WORKING

Prepare a braid using the above details. Thread the finished braid through the beads so that the large bead is hanging vertically (see instructions on page 23).

SAMPLE 2C

BEAD DETAILS:

1 'Spacer' - gold plated metal
    Bead size: 5mm(³⁄₁₆in) Hole size: 4mm(⁵⁄₃₂in)
1 'Large' - painted ceramic
    Bead size: 25mm(1in) Hole size: 5mm(³⁄₁₆in)

BRAID DETAILS:

Braiding sequence: Spiral Braid One
Bobbin weight: 70gms (2½oz)
Weight bag: 275gms (10oz)
Finished length: 80cm (31½in)

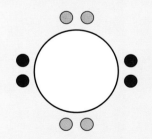

WARP DETAILS:

◒ 8 strands of grey silk, 1.35m (53in) long
◒ 8 strands of blue silk, 1.35m (53in) long
● 16 strands of navy silk, 1.35m (53in) long

WORKING

Prepare a braid using the above details. Thread the finished braid through the beads so that the large bead is hanging horizontally (see instructions on page 23).

3 THREADING -KNOTTED

An attractive way of preventing beads from slipping along a braid is to knot the braid between the beads. With such a range of different knots, the possibilities are endless. From the simple elegance of the overhand knot (see below), to the complex decoration of the Chinese knots (see page 4).

SAMPLE 3A

BEAD DETAILS:

16 'Tubes' - iridescent glass
Bead size: 3mm(⅛in) Hole size: 2mm(⅜₄in)

BRAID DETAILS:

Braiding sequence: Square Braid

Bobbin weight: 37gms (1⅓oz)

Weight bag: 150gms (5¼oz)

Finished length: 50cm (20in)

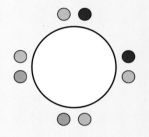

WARP DETAILS:

● 4 strands of purple silk, 1.35m (53in) long

● 4 strands of green silk, 1.35m (53in) long

● 4 strands of lilac silk, 1.35m (53in) long

WORKING

Make a braid using the instructions above.

   Thread one bead on to the finished braid and position it close to one end. Tie two overhand knots in the braid, one each side of the bead (See Fig. 3.1). Repeat this procedure along the braid, spacing the beads out at intervals of approximately 4cm (1½)ins.

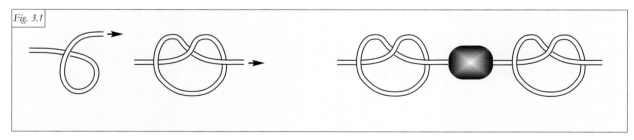

Fig. 3.1

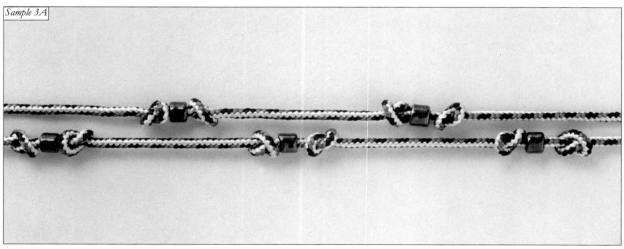

Sample 3A

3. THREADING-KNOTTED

SAMPLE 3B

BRAID DETAILS:

Braiding sequence: Square Braid

Bobbin weight: 37gms (1⅓oz)

Weight bag: 150gms (5¼oz)

Finished length: 35cm (14in)

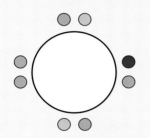

BEAD DETAILS:

24 'Tubes' - iridescent glass
   Bead size: 3mm(⅛in) Hole size: 2mm(⁵⁄₆₄in)
12 'Charms' - miscellaneous metal shapes
   Bead size: 20mm(²⁵⁄₃₂in) Hole size: 2mm(⁵⁄₆₄in)

WARP DETAILS:

● 4 strands of purple silk, 1.35m (53in) long

● 4 strands of green silk, 1.35m (53in) long

○ 4 strands of lilac silk, 1.35m (53) long

WORKING

Prepare a square braid using the details shown.

Thread a bead, a charm pendant and another bead on to one end of the braid. Now use both ends of the braid to tie a reef knot above the cluster of three beads (See Fig. 3.2).

Add another cluster of three (bead, charm, bead) and tie another reef knot above these. This time use the non-beaded end of the braid to make most of the knotting. This reduces the risk of tangling the beads already added. Continue until all the beads have been added.

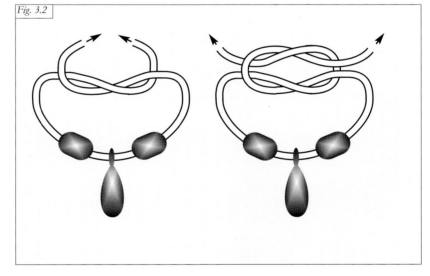

Fig. 3.2

Sample 3B

3. THREADING-KNOTTED

SAMPLE 3C

BEAD DETAILS:

16 'Tubes' - iridescent glass
   Bead size: 3mm(⅛in) Hole size: 2mm(⁵⁄₆₄in)
8 'Charms' - miscellaneous metal shapes
   Bead size:20mm(²⁵⁄₃₂in) Hole size: 2mm(⁵⁄₆₄in)

BRAID DETAILS:

Braiding sequence: Square Braid
Bobbin weight: 37gms (1⅓oz)
Weight bag: 150gms 5¼oz)
Finished length: 20cm (8in)

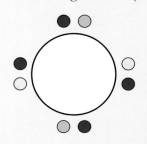

WARP DETAILS:

● 4 strands of purple silk, 1.35m (53in) long
○ 4 strands of grey silk, 1.35m (53in) long
◐ 4 strands of lilac silk, 1.35m (53in) long

WORKING

Make a loose overhand knot close to the end of the finished braid. Add a bead, a charm and another bead. Tie another, loose, overhand knot approximately 75mm (3in) along the braid.

(Make sure that the cluster of beads remains between the two knots). Add another set of three beads and tie another loose knot 75mm(3in) from the last. Continue adding clusters of

beads and tying loose knots.

When the last of the beads have been added, take the end of the braid back through each knot and tighten (see Fig 3.3).

Detail of Sample 3C

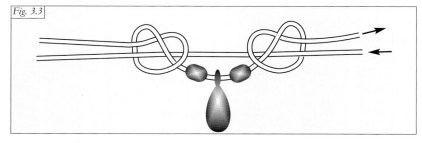

Fig. 3.3

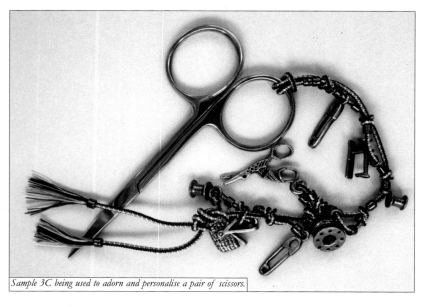

Sample 3C being used to adorn and personalise a pair of scissors.

4 THREADING - MULTI

So far we have only looked at threading beads on to one braid. However, by using two (or more!) braids, new ideas can be played with. Each sample

requires two braids. Both are square braids but have different surface patterns. This is achieved by working a braid from each of the coloured starting positions

shown in the table. When the braids have been completed they can both be threaded through the beads.

SAMPLE 4A

BRAID DETAILS:

Braiding sequence: Square Braid
Bobbin weight: 70gms (2½oz)
Weight bag: 275gms (10oz)
Finished length: 35cm (14in)

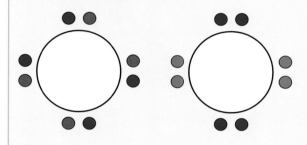

BEAD DETAILS:

6 'Spacers' - gold plated metal
Bead size: 5mm(¾₆in) Hole size: 4mm(⅚₂in)

WARP DETAILS:

● 10 strands of purple silk, 66cm (26in) long
● 10 strands of pink silk, 66cm (26in) long
● 10 strands of blue silk, 66cm (26in) long

WORKING

For this sample the braids enter the beads from opposite directions creating a circular lacing effect (See Fig. 4.1).
Just six beads are used. The amount of braid between adjacent beads is gradually diminished. Finally, the ends of both braids are whipped together to complete the piece.

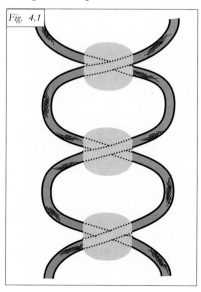

Fig. 4.1

Sample 4A detail

Sample 4A

SAMPLE 4B

BRAID DETAILS:

Braiding sequence: Square Braid

Bobbin weight: 70gms (2½oz)

Weight bag: 275gms (10oz)

Finished length: 70cm (27½in)

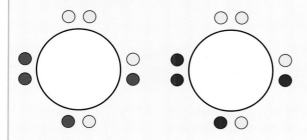

BEAD DETAILS:

25 'Spacers' - gold plated metal
Bead size: 5mm(³/₁₆in) Hole size: 4mm(⁵/₃₂in)

WARP DETAILS:

● 10 strands of purple silk,
1.35m (53in) long

● 10 strands of pink silk,
1.35m (53in) long

○ 6 strands of gold Metallic Biron,
1.35m (53in) long

WORKING

For this example the two braids are threaded through the beads in alternate ways.

Firstly both braids go through the beads in the same direction. Then the braids split and enter the bead from opposite ends. By alternating the threading procedure in this way a figure eight style of lacing is achieved (See Fig.4.2).

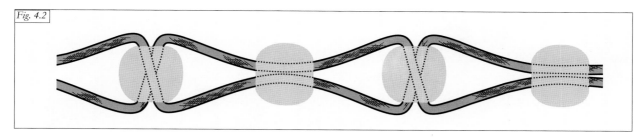

Fig. 4.2

Sample 4B

SAMPLE 4C

BRAID DETAILS:

Braiding sequence: Square Braid
Bobbin weight: 70gms (2½oz)
Weight bag: 275gms (10oz)
Finished length: 60cm (23½in)

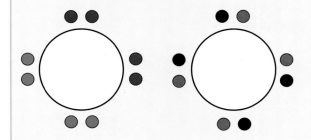

BEAD DETAILS:

25 'Spacers' - gold plated metal
    Bead size: 5mm(³⁄₁₆in) Hole size: 4mm(⁵⁄₃₂in)

WARP DETAILS:

- 14 strands of purple silk,
    1.35m (53in) long
- 14 strands of blue silk,
    1.35m (53in) long
- 6 strands of purple silk,
    1.35m (53in) long
- 6 strands of pink silk,
    1.35m (53in) long

WORKING

Here the braids are laced
through the beads in the same
manner as Sample 4B. However,
the two different sizes of braid
produce a quite different effect.

Sample 4C

5 THREADING-THROUGH

The unique structure of the ladder braid allows for the strings of beads to be threaded through the braid, rather than on to it.

Different results are obtained by taking the strings of beads in and out of the braid slits in different directions.

The beads are prepared on an extra long piece of thread. This allows for the ends of the thread to be sewn into the braid.

You may wish to put a temporary knot in the end of the thread to stop the beads from falling off. But do remember to remove it before sewing the thread in to the braid.

SAMPLE 5A

BRAID DETAILS:

Braiding sequence: Ladder Braid

Bobbin weight: 70gms (2½oz)

Weight bag: 250gms (8¾oz)

Finished length: 160cm (63in)

BEAD DETAILS:

190cm(75in) String of iridescent red rocaille
Bead size: 8/0

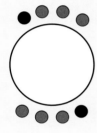

WARP DETAILS:

● 20 strands of black silk, 2.7m (9ft) long

● 20 strands of red silk, 2.7m (9ft) long

WORKING

Separately prepare a ladder braid and a string of beads using the details above.

Start by sewing one end of the bead string into the beginning of the braid. Try to conceal the stitches as neatly as possible. When the string of beads is secure, take the other end through each braid slit in turn. The beads go under and over the slits following the path shown (See Fig. 5.1).

When all the slits have been laced through, sew the end of the bead string into the end of the braid.

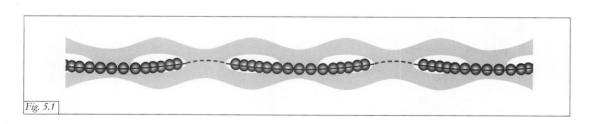

Fig. 5.1

Sample 5A

SAMPLE 5B

BRAID DETAILS:

Braiding sequence: Ladder Braid

Bobbin weight: 70gms (2½oz)

Weight bag: 250gms (8¾oz)

Finished length: 160cm (63in)

BEAD DETAILS:

260cm(102in) String of iridescent red rocaille
Bead size: 8/0

WARP DETAILS:

● 20 strands of black silk, 2.7m (9ft) long

● 20 strands of red silk, 2.7m (9ft) long

○ 20 strands of pink silk, 2.7m (9ft) long

WORKING

Use the details above to produce a ladder braid and string of beads. Attach the two together as discussed in Sample 5A.

Now lace the beads through the braid so that they zig zag from side to side (See Fig 5.2).

Fig. 5.2

Sample 5B

5. THREADING-THROUGH

SAMPLE 5C

BRAID DETAILS:

Braiding sequence: Ladder Braid

Bobbin weight: 70gms (2½oz)

Weight bag: 250gms (8¾oz)

Finished length: 160cm (63in)

BEAD DETAILS:

250cm(98in) String of metallic grey rocaille.
Bead size: 8/0

WARP DETAILS:

⬤ 20 strands of red silk, 2.7m (9ft) long

◯ 20 strands of pink silk, 2.7m (9ft) long

WORKING

This sample follows the same idea as used in Samples 5A and 5B, except that the beads are laced through following a different route (See Fig 5.3).
This causes the sample to have a distinctive twist.

Fig 5.3

Sample 5C

6 SEWING-RANDOM

One of the most efficient and effective ways of embellishing is to use a needle and thread to sew beads on to a finished braid. As the relationship between bead hole and braid is irrelevant, the range of possibilities is enormous. The sewing stitches can be effectively concealed by working with threads similar to those used for the braiding and ensuring that they are carefully placed to hide themselves in the braid stitches.

Samples 6A, B & C

SAMPLE 6A

BRAID DETAILS:

Braiding sequence: Flat Braid Two

Bobbin weight: 100gms (3½oz)

Weight bag: 375gms (13oz)

Finished length: 55cm (22in)

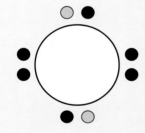

BEAD DETAILS:

Approximately 150 metallic red rocaille
    Bead size: 8/0

WARP DETAILS:

● 40 strands of black Biron, 1.35m (53in) long

◯ 40 strands of yellow Biron, 1.35m (53in) long

WORKING

Complete the flat braid as detailed.

Using a length of black Biron, sew a couple of stitches into the braid to secure its end. Now sew the needle and thread randomly through the braid. Every time it comes out of the braid, add a bead on to the thread before returning the needle back into the braid, close to where it exited. When sufficient beads have been added, make a couple of plain stitches on top of each other to secure the end.

Sample 6A

SAMPLE 6B

BRAID DETAILS:

Braiding sequence: Flat Braid Two

Bobbin weight: 100gms (3½oz)

Weight bag: 375gms (13oz)

Finished length: 55cm (22in)

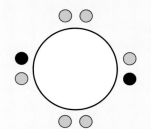

BEAD DETAILS:

60 'Round' - gold plated metal
Bead size: 2mm(⁵⁄₆₄in)
60 'Bugle' - gold plated metal
Beads size: 5x1mm(³⁄₁₆x³⁄₆₄in)

WARP DETAILS:

● 40 strands of black Biron, 1.35m (53in) long

○ 40 strands of yellow Biron, 1.35m (53in) long

WORKING

Add the beads in the same way as Sample 6A except group together clusters of bugles and round beads.

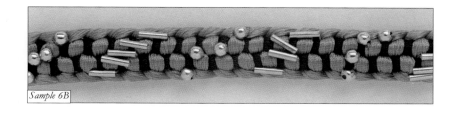

Sample 6B

SAMPLE 6C

BRAID DETAILS:

Braiding sequence: Flat Braid Two

Bobbin weight: 100gms (3½oz)

Weight bag: 375gms (13oz)

Finished length: 110cm (43in)

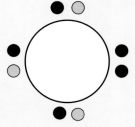

BEAD DETAILS:

60 Pearl Buttons
Bead size: 10mm(¹³⁄₃₂in)

WARP DETAILS:

● 40 strands of black Biron, 2.7m (9ft) long

○ 40 strands of yellow Biron, 2.7m (9ft) long

WORKING

Randomly sew small pearl buttons on to the finished braid.

Sample 6C

7 SEWING-PATTERNED

Beads can be sewn on in a more orderly fashion by using the structure of the braid as a guide. Here the needle and thread can run through the braid, exiting at particular points along the braid. Beads can be added to the thread before the needle is returned into the braid again using the braid stitches as a guide for the entry point.

Sample 7A in progress.

Samples 7 A, B & C.

7. SEWING-PATTERNED

SAMPLE 7A

BRAID DETAILS:

Braiding sequence: Rectangular Braid

Bobbin weight: 100gms (3½oz)

Weight bag: 375gms (13oz)

Finished length: 140cm (55in)

BEAD DETAILS:

200 'Round' - gold plated metal
Bead size: 2mm(⁵⁄₆₄in)

WARP DETAILS:

- ● 40 strands of black Biron, 2.7m (9ft) long
- ● 40 strands of green Biron, 2.7m (9ft) long
- ○ 40 strands of pale green Biron, 2.7m (59ft) long

WORKING

The gold beads are sewn into the 'dimples' of this rectangular braid. Work with a thread similar to those used in the warp to help conceal the stitches. The needle and thread travel along the inside of the braid in a central, straight line. The needle must exit the braid at the join of the braid stitches. A small gold bead is added before the needle returns into the braid close to the point of exit (See Fig 7.1).

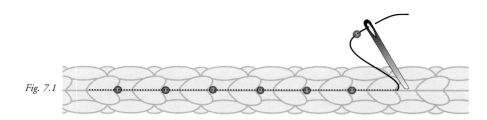

Fig. 7.1

Sample 7A

SAMPLE 7B

BRAID DETAILS:

Braiding sequence: Rectangular Braid

Bobbin weight: 100gms (3½oz)

Weight bag: 375gms (13oz)

Finished length: 140cm (55in)

BEAD DETAILS:

400 'Round' - gold plated metal
Bead size: 2mm(⁵⁄₆₄in)

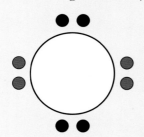

WARP DETAILS:

● 40 strands of black Biron, 2.7m (9ft) long

● 40 strands of green Biron, 2.7m (9ft) long

WORKING

Here the needle and thread zigzag from one edge of the braid to the other. A single bead is added on each side at the point where the needle exits and turns back into the braid. Work one line of zigzags along the braid (See Fig. 7.2). Then repeat a similar line of zigzags so that the gold beads sit in regular spots along both edges of the braid (See Fig. 7.3).

Fig. 7.2

Fig. 7.3

Sample 7B

7. SEWING-PATTERNED

SAMPLE 7C

BRAID DETAILS:

Braiding sequence: Rectangular Braid

Bobbin weight: 100gms (3½oz)

Weight bag: 375gms (13oz)

Finished length: 140cm (55in)

BEAD DETAILS:

1000 black rocaille
Bead size: 8/0

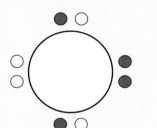

WARP DETAILS:

⬤ 40 strands of green Biron, 2.7m (9ft) long

◯ 40 strands of pale green Biron, 2.7m (9ft) long

WORKING

Again the needle and thread travel from one edge of the braid to the other but this time the angle of the thread inside the braid is perpendicular to the edge. As the needle exits the braid, five black beads are added. The needle returns back into the braid at a point further along the edge (See Fig. 7.4).

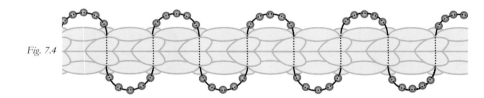

Fig. 7.4

Sample 7C

8 SEWING-PENDANT

Larger beads can also be sewn on to a finished braid. Here pendants are sewn on to a braid to produce a necklace.

By using thread similar to the warp, the join can become an integral part of the design.

SAMPLE 8A

BRAID DETAILS:

Braiding sequence: Spiral Braid Two

Bobbin weight: 70gms (2½oz)

Weight bag: 275gms (10oz)

Finished length: 80cm (31½in)

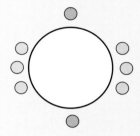

BEAD DETAILS:

1 'Pendant' - polymer clay disc
Bead size: 20mm($^{25}/_{32}$in)

WARP DETAILS:

● 20 strands of ochre silk, 1.35m (53in) long
○ 20 strands of blue silk, 1.35m (53in) long

WORKING

Carefully sew a couple of small securing stitches into the finished braid at a point where you want the bead to hang. Take the needle and thread through the bead hole and back into the braid (See Fig 8.1).

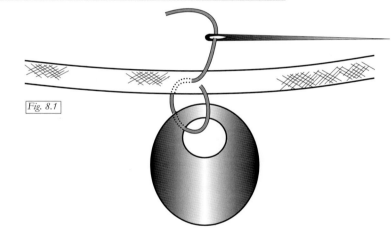

Fig. 8.1

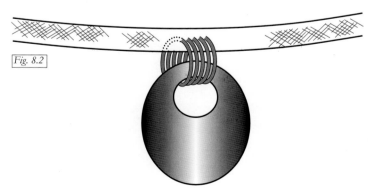

Fig. 8.2

Sample 8A

Position the bead so that it is butting up against the braid. Continue stitching through the bead and the braid. Try to keep the stitches neat and parallel to each other. Finish with a couple of small securing stitches (See Fig 8.2).

8. SEWING-PENDANT

SAMPLE 8B

BRAID DETAILS:

Braiding sequence: Spiral Braid Two

Bobbin weight: 70gms (2½oz)

Weight bag: 275gms (10oz)

Finished length: 80cm (31½in)

BEAD DETAILS:

1 'Pendant' - polymer clay disc

Bead size: 25mm(1in)

WARP DETAILS:

○ 20 strands of ochre silk, 1.35m (53in) long

● 20 strands of navy silk, 1.35m (53in) long

WORKING

Sew the bead on to the braid in the same manner as Sample 8A. However, before finishing, take the thread a couple of times around all of the stitches between the braid and the top of the bead. This whipping of thread perpendicular to the joining stitches gives a tighter, neater join (See Fig 8.3).

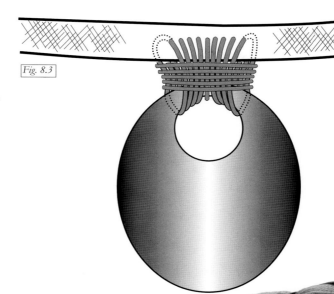

Fig. 8.3

Sample 8B

SAMPLE 8C

BRAID DETAILS:

Braiding sequence: Spiral Braid Two

Bobbin weight: 70gms (2½oz)

Weight bag: 275gms (10oz)

Finished length: 80cm (31½in)

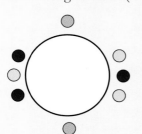

BEAD DETAILS:

1 'Pendant' - polymer clay disc
Bead size: 20mm(²⁵⁄₃₂in)

WARP DETAILS:

- 20 strands of ochre silk, 1.35m (53in) long
- 20 strands of blue silk, 1.35m (53in) long
- 20 strands of navy silk, 1.35m (53in) long

WORKING

This sample takes the sewing a step further. The bead is added as shown in Sample 8A. When the joining stitches are complete, take the needle and thread around them making a series of little half hitches over the top (See Fig 8.4).

Work over the back and front sections to create a fancy finish to the join.

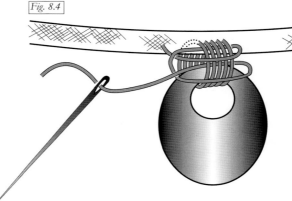

Fig. 8.4

Sample 8C

9 SEWING-CONNECTING

Although this is another method using needle and thread, it can be thought of as adding the braid to a string of beads as opposed to adding the beads to the braid. For this reason it is preferable to use normal beading thread rather than warp threads so that the emphasis is on strength rather than disguise.

SAMPLE 9A

BRAID DETAILS:

Braiding sequence: Round Braid Two

Bobbin weight: 70gms (2½oz)

Weight bag: 325gms (11½oz)

Finished length: 55cm (22in)

BEAD DETAILS:

50 black faceted glass
    Bead size: 8mm(⁵⁄₁₆in)

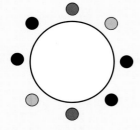

WARP DETAILS:

- ● 20 strands of black Biron, 2.7m (9ft) long
- ● 20 strands of red Biron, 2.7m (9ft) long
- ○ 20 strands of orange Biron, 2.7m (9ft) long

WORKING

Make a braid using the details shown. Whip the ends of the braid and secure a length of beading thread into the start of the braid. Use a beading needle to thread a black bead on to this beading thread. Now take the needle and thread straight through the braid, a short distance from the start. Add another bead before taking the needle and thread through the braid again.

Continue threading the beads and braid together. (See Fig.9.1) A meandering effect is achieved by altering the distance between each exit and entrance point of the needle.

Fig. 9.1

Sample 9A

9. SEWING-CONNECTING

SAMPLE 9B

BEAD DETAILS:

40 red faceted glass
Bead size: 8mm(⁵⁄₁₆in)
80 black round glass
Bead size: 4mm(⁵⁄₃₂in)

BRAID DETAILS:

Braiding sequence: Round Braid Two
Bobbin weight: 70gms (2½oz)
Weight bag: 325gms (11½oz)
Finished length: 75cm (29½in)

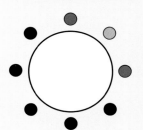

WARP DETAILS:

● 20 strands of black Biron, 2.7m (9ft) long
● 20 strands of red Biron, 2.7m (9ft) long
○ 20 strands of orange Biron, 2.7m (9ft) long

WORKING

Here a series of three beads (black, red and black) are added on to the beading thread. The beading needle and thread is taken through the braid at a set distance along the braid 4cm (1½in). This should equate to five pattern repeats on the braid.

Sample 9B

9. SEWING-CONNECTING

SAMPLE 9C

BRAID DETAILS:

Braiding sequence: Round Braid Two

Bobbin weight: 70gms (2½oz)

Weight bag: 325gms (11½oz)

Finished length: 75cm (29½in)

BEAD DETAILS:

24 black faceted glass
    Bead size: 8mm(⁵⁄₁₆in)
1 red faceted glass
    Bead size: 10mm(¹³⁄₃₂in)
2 each of the following sized red faceted glass
    Bead size: 3mm(⅛in), 4mm(⁵⁄₃₂in),
    5mm(³⁄₁₆in), 6mm(¼in), 8mm(⁵⁄₁₆in)

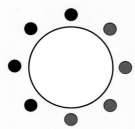

WARP DETAILS:

● 20 strands of black Biron, 2.7m (9ft) long

● 20 strands of red Biron, 2.7m (9ft) long

WORKING

Start approximately 22cm(8½in) from one end and work a section of the meandering effect created in Sample 9A.

When twelve black beads have been threaded on, add five red beads in graduated sizes (smallest first). Go through the braid and add the single, largest red bead. Now take the needle and thread through the braid at a distance of approx 18cm(7in) before working the other half of the necklace in a mirror image of the first half.

Sample 9C

10 BELL-CAPS

This way of combining beads and braids is particularly adaptable. Bell cap ends are metal fittings that can be placed on to the ends of braids. Beads, threaded on to eyepin links, can then be attached on to these bell caps. This technique is especially useful for large beads with small holes that are difficult to use in other circumstances.

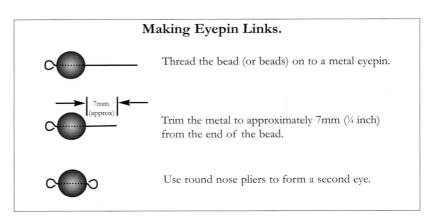

Making Eyepin Links.

Thread the bead (or beads) on to a metal eyepin.

7mm (approx)

Trim the metal to approximately 7mm (¼ inch) from the end of the bead.

Use round nose pliers to form a second eye.

Bell caps also provide natural ends and joins, giving options for other jewellery fittings to be used.

A clasp and jump ring forming a join between two bell caps.

SAMPLE 10A

BEAD DETAILS:

2 'Bell caps' - brass, with eyepin
    Hole size: 5mm(³⁄₁₆in)
1 'Pendant' - gold plated pendant with eyepin link
    Bead size: 25mm(1in)

BRAID DETAILS:

Braiding sequence: Round Braid One

Bobbin weight: 100gms (3½oz)

Weight bag: 375gms (13oz)

Finished length: 70cm (27½in)

WARP DETAILS:

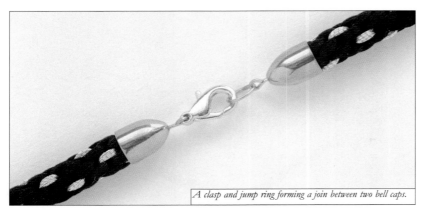

● 40 strands of black Biron, 1.35m (53in) long

○ 30 strands of gold metallic Biron, 1.35m (53in) long

WORKING

Make a braid using the details shown. Securely whip both ends as usual. At the centre of the braid make a pair of small, tight whippings with a small gap between them. Cut the braid in half, slicing between the two central whippings. The whippings prevent the sections of braid from unravelling.

Now trim away any loose threads from these two points.

Make the ends as neat as possible so that they will be well hidden under the bell cap.

10. BELL-CAPS

Apply some suitable adhesive on to the ends of the braid and cover them with the bell caps. Wait until the glue is dry before adding the pendant bead.

Ease open the eyes on the link and place them through the eyes on the bell caps. Close the eyes by returning the wire to its original circular position.

Parts of Sample 10A

Sample 10A

SAMPLE 10B

BRAID DETAILS:

Braiding sequence: Round Braid One

Bobbin weight: 100gms (3½oz)

Weight bag: 375gms (13oz)

Finished length: 90cm (35½in)

WARP DETAILS:

● 40 strands of black Biron, 1.35m (53in) long

○ 30 strands of gold metallic Biron, 1.35m (53in) long

BEAD DETAILS:

20 'Bell caps' - brass, with eyepin
      Hole size: 5mm(³⁄₁₆in)

10 black Cloisonne with eyepin link
      Bead size: 12mm(¹⁵⁄₃₂in)

WORKING

Make a braid from the details above.

Now the braid needs to be prepared so that it can be cut into sections. At a point 6cm (2¼in) in from one end, make a pair of small, tight whippings with a small gap between them.

Measure along the braid another 6cm (2¼in) before making another pair of whippings. Each time you measure along the braid you are producing one more braid section for the final piece. When you have sewn off the braid into ten sections, cut between the

pairs of whippings and trim the ends. Glue a bell cap on to both ends of every braid section and allow to dry. Complete the piece by using a single bead on a wire eyepin link to connect each braid section.

Sample 10B

10. BELL-CAPS

SAMPLE 10C

BRAID DETAILS:

Braiding sequence: Round Braid One

Bobbin weight: 100gms (3½oz)

Weight bag: 375gms (13oz)

Finished length: 100cm (39in)

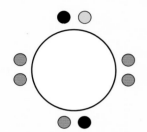

BEAD DETAILS:

20 'Bell caps' - brass, with eyepin
 Hole size: 5mm($\frac{3}{16}$in)

10 'Amber' - acrylic
 Bead size: 18mm($\frac{23}{32}$in)

20 black round glass
 Bead size: 8mm($\frac{5}{16}$in)

WARP DETAILS:

● 40 strands of black Biron, 1.35m (53in) long

○ 30 strands of gold metallic Biron, 1.35m (53in) long

● 40 strands of rust Biron, 1.35 (53in) long

WORKING

Follow the working method described in Sample 10B, except connect the braid sections together with a wire eyepin link threaded with a set of three beads (black, amber and black).

Sample 10C

11 TWISTS

Twisting a string of beads around a braid can be a simple way of combining the two together. However, care must be taken to ensure that the match is suitable and that the beads are tightly wrapped around the braid. The following samples use the spiral structured braid that gives a natural trough in which the beads can sit. By filling just one of the double helixes plenty of the braid remains visible to complement the beads

SAMPLE 11A

BRAID DETAILS:

Braiding sequence: Spiral Braid Two

Bobbin weight: 70gms (2½oz)

Weight bag: 250gms (8¾oz)

Finished length: 140cm (55in)

BEAD DETAILS:

160cm(63in) String of green iridescent rocaille
Bead size: 8/0

WARP DETAILS:

- 20 strands of green silk, 2.7m (9ft) long
- 20 strands of burgundy silk, 2.7m (9ft) long
- 20 strands of cream silk, 2.7m (9ft) long

WORKING

Sew one end of the bead string into the beginning of the braid. Slowly wrap the string of beads around the braid allowing the beads to sit in the inner core of the spiral. Keep the string of beads tight against the braid. It is better to pull the beads too tight than too slack. This will prevent the beads from sagging down away from the braid when the piece is finished. When the beads arrive at the end of the braid, sew the end of the bead string into the braid to secure.

Twisting the string of beads around the braid.

Sample 11A

SAMPLE 11B

BRAID DETAILS:

Braiding sequence: Spiral Braid Two
Bobbin weight: 70gms (2½oz)
Weight bag: 250gms (8¾oz)
Finished length: 140cm (55in)

BEAD DETAILS:

160cm (63in) String of green iridescent rocaille
Bead size: 8/0

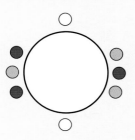

WARP DETAILS:

- 20 strands of green silk, 2.7m (9ft) long
- 20 strands of light green silk, 2.7m (9ft) long
- 20 strands of cream silk, 2.7m (9ft) long

WORKING: As Sample 11A

Sample 11B

SAMPLE 11C

BRAID DETAILS:

Braiding sequence: Spiral Braid Two
Bobbin weight: 70gms (2½oz)
Weight bag: 250gms (8¾oz)
Finished length: 140cm (55in)

BEAD DETAILS:

160cm (63in) String of green iridescent rocaille
Bead size: 8/0

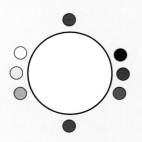

WARP DETAILS:

- 20 strands of green silk, 2.7m (9ft) long
- 20 strands of dark burgundy silk, 2.7m (9ft) long
- 20 strands of burgundy silk, 2.7m (9ft) long
- 20 strands of dark pink silk, 2.7m (9ft) long
- 20 strands of pink silk, 2.7m (9ft) long
- 20 strands of pale pink silk, 2.7m (9ft) long
- 20 strands of cream silk, 2.7m (9ft) long

WORKING: As Sample 11A

Sample 11C

12 WIREWORK

Taking a fine wire through beads and braids can produce unusual effects. The wire needs to be soft and pliable to allow for easy working but firm enough to hold its shape. Care should be taken to keep the wire straight or in smooth curves. This prevents kinks forming in the wire that are difficult to remove.

The braids used in the samples are made with a loose tension. This should be sufficient to allow the wire to be pushed between the stitches. If this proves difficult, use a darning needle to 'sew' the wire through the braid. A small pair of pliers can also be useful to handle the end of the wire.

You may also find it easier to work on a cork or polystyrene board. Pinning the piece of work on to a board will help give a more even layout.

Work always starts at the centre of the braid. This means less wire has to be pulled through the braid. At the ends of the braid the wire can be knotted or sewn over to secure.

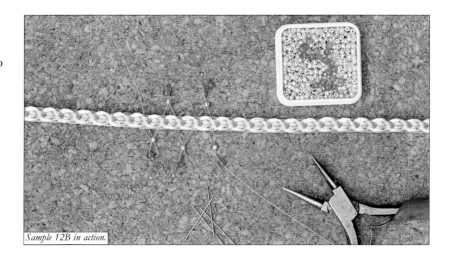

Sample 12B in action.

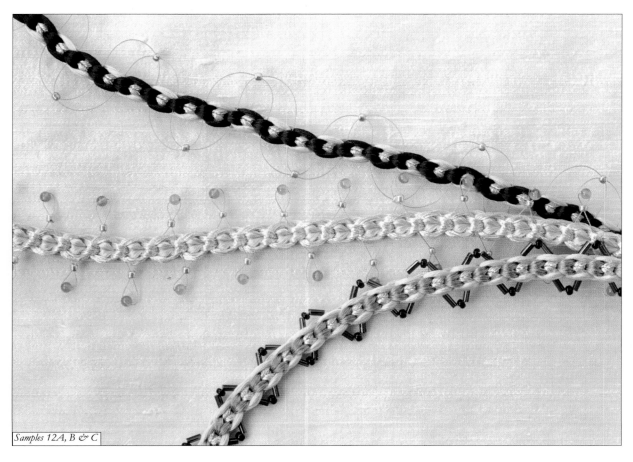

Samples 12A, B & C

12. WIREWORK

SAMPLE 12A

BRAID DETAILS:

Braiding sequence: Rectangular Braid

Bobbin weight: 100gms (3½oz)

Weight bag: 450gms (16oz)

Finished length: 75cm (29½in)

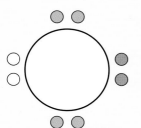

BEAD DETAILS:

180 blue, silver lined bugles
    Bead size: 5x2mm(³⁄₁₆x⁵⁄₆₄in)
90 blue rocaille
    Beads size: 8/0
120cm (47¼in) Nylon coated wire cable 0.01cm thick

WARP DETAILS:

🔵 40 strands of light blue Biron, 1.35m (53in) long

⚫ 40 strands of grey Biron, 1.35m (53in) long

⚪ 30 strands of silver metallised Biron, 1.35m (53in) long

WORKING

Start at the centre of the finished braid. Thread the wire through the braid taking it from one edge to the other. Pull it through until the centre of the wire is reached. Thread a set of three beads (bugle, rocaille, bugle) on to the wire. Push the wire back through the braid following the path shown in Fig 12.1. Continue working until one half of the braid has been beaded. Go back to the centre of the braid and start working in the opposite direction to the other end of the braid.

Fig.12.1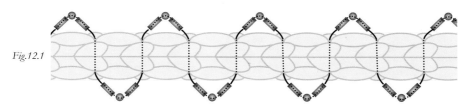

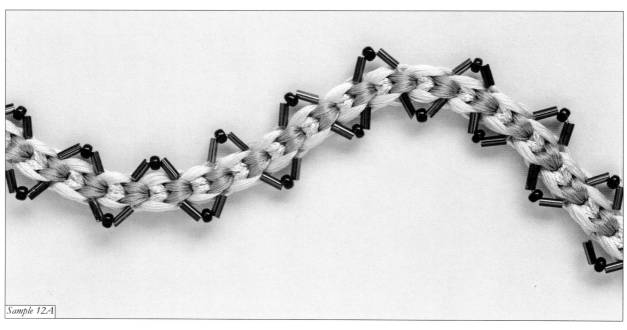

Sample 12A

SAMPLE 12B

BEAD DETAILS:

100 semi-precious stone - blue agate
    Bead size: 3mm(⅛in)
100 metallic silver rocaille
    Beads size: 8/0
4m (13ft) Nylon coated wire cable 0.01cm thick

BRAID DETAILS:

Braiding sequence: Rectangular Braid

Bobbin weight: 100gms (3½oz)

Weight bag: 450gms (16oz)

Finished length: 80cm (31½in)

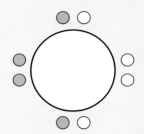

WARP DETAILS:

⬤ 40 strands of light blue Biron, 1.35m (53in) long

◯ 30 strands of silver metallised Biron, 1.35m (53in) long

WORKING

Here the wire holds the beads away from the edge of the braid (approximately 12mm(½in) from the edge). Start at the centre of the braid. Thread the wire through the braid stitch until the centre of the wire is reached.

Add one silver and one blue bead. Now take the wire back through the silver bead. Thread the wire through the next stitch of the braid and out to the opposite edge (See Fig 12.2).

Continue beading in the same manner until the end of the braid is reached. Go back to the centre of the braid and start working in the opposite direction to the other end of the braid.

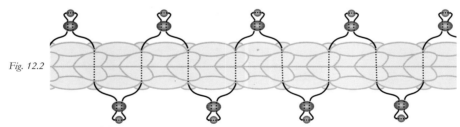

Fig. 12.2

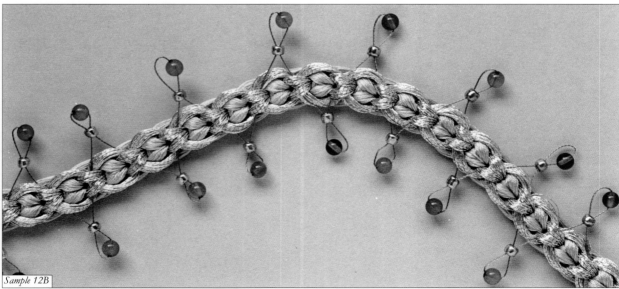

Sample 12B

12. WIREWORK

SAMPLE 12C

BRAID DETAILS:

Braiding sequence: Rectangular Braid

Bobbin weight: 100gms (3½oz)

Weight bag: 450gms (16oz)

Finished length: 75cm (29½in)

BEAD DETAILS:

40 silver metallic rocaille
    Beads size: 8/0

2x 2m (12½ft) Nylon coated wire cable
    0.01cm thick

WARP DETAILS:

🔘 40 strands of light blue Biron, 1.35m (53in) long

⚫ 40 strands of blue Biron, 1.35m (53in) long

⚪ 30 strands of silver metallised Biron, 1.35m (53in) long

WORKING

As always, start at the centre of the braid. Thread the first wire through until the centre of the wire is reached. Add a bead and pass the wire back through the braid to the opposite edge. Do not pull the wire all the way. Leave enough wire so that the bead is sitting on an arc of wire approximately 1cm(½in) from the edge. Keep repeating this manoeuvre until the wire has laced its way along the braid, adding beads on each side (See Fig 12.3).

Insert the second piece of wire through the braid, one braid stitch off-centre (See Fig 12.4). Take the end of the wire through the closest bead before taking it back through the braid to the opposite side. Keep lacing the second wire through the beads and braid until complete.

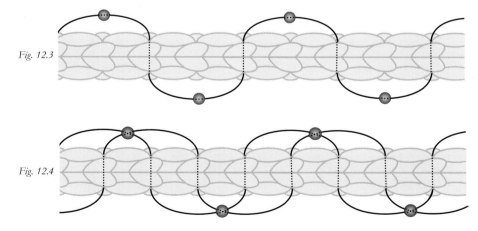

Fig. 12.3

Fig. 12.4

Sample 12C

GALLERY 1

Necklace made from spherical, lattice beads threaded on to the finished braids

A hand-turned brass bead loop
threaded on to a silk braid.

These beautiful hand-made glass beads are complemented
by a fine silk braid threaded and knotted through them.

A necklace made from several silk braids threaded through a selection of lampwork beads.

GALLERY 5

Two examples of beads threaded through split braids.

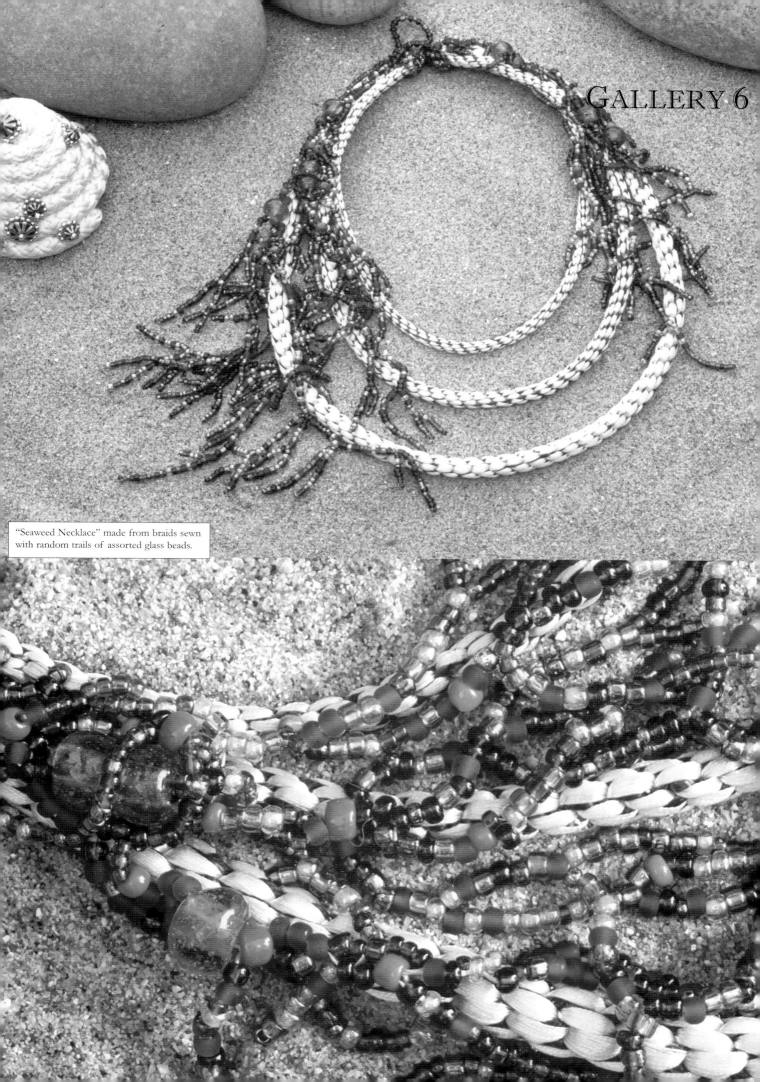

"Seaweed Necklace" made from braids sewn with random trails of assorted glass beads.

GALLERY 7

Bugle and Rocaille beads sewn into the spiral
braid to form a "Spiney Norman" bracelet.

GALLERY 8

Lampwork pendant with a silk tassel sewn on to a distorted beaded braid.

GALLERY 9

Black Onyx beads sewn through a tapered braid
to form the connecting loops of the necklace.

GALLERY 10

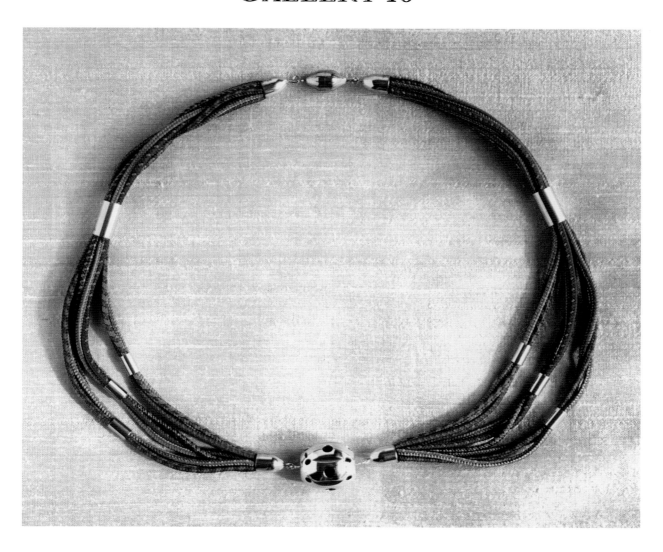

Necklace made with hand-turned
brass bead, tubes and bell caps.

GALLERY 11

A string of Mother of Pearl beads
twisted around a finished braid.

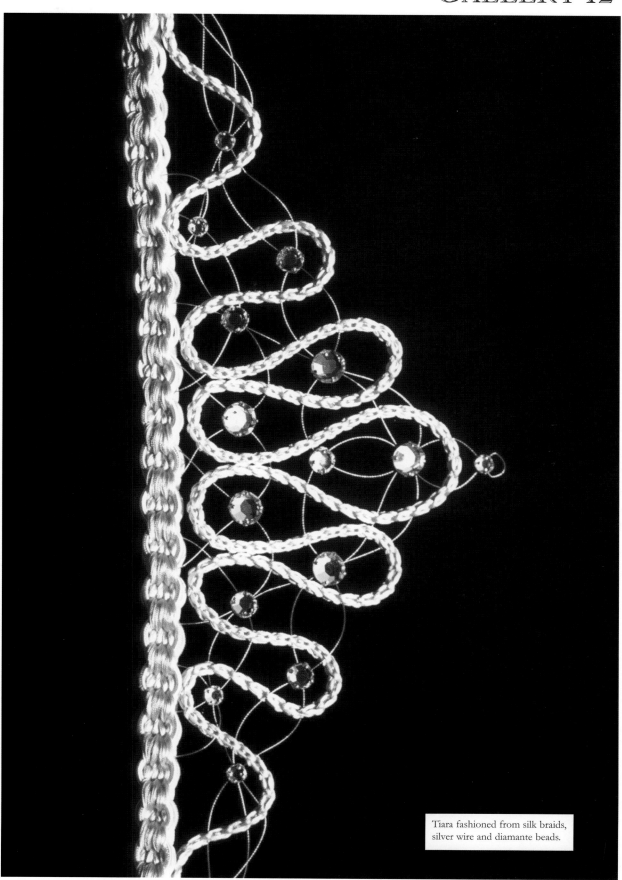

Tiara fashioned from silk braids, silver wire and diamante beads.

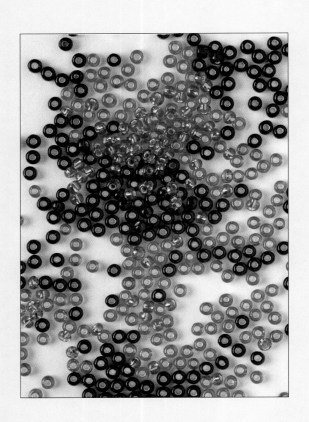

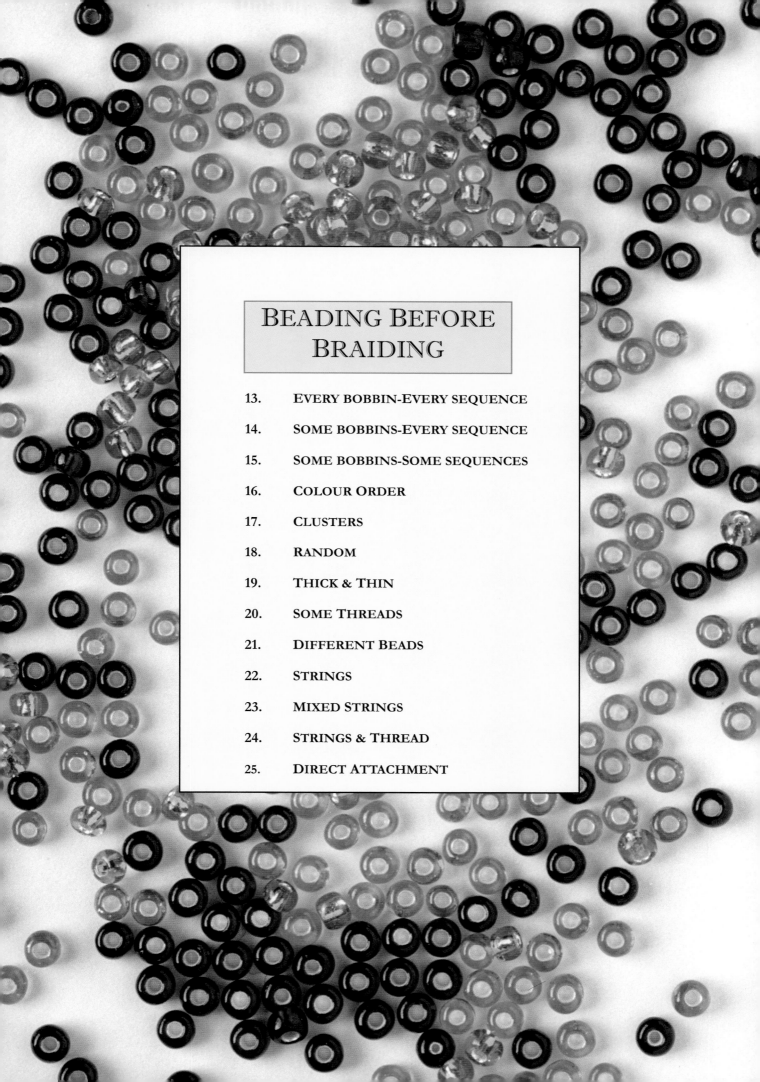

BEADING BEFORE BRAIDING

13 EVERY BOBBIN-EVERY SEQUENCE

These samples use rocaille beads threaded on to the warp threads before braiding starts. The beads are pushed into the point of braiding during the braiding process to produce rich, densely beaded results.

The braid needs to be of a sufficient scale to provide the underlying structure for the beads to sit on. To this end the maximum number of warp threads are taken through the beads. However, the amount of warp threads used may have to be varied to compensate for the irregular hole sizes found with these types of beads (discussed on page 10).

In order to get the maximum number of threads through the beads, a leading thread is used (see Fig 13.1). The leading thread allows the beads to pass separately over the eye of the needle and the bulk of the warp threads. An alternative is to cover the warp threads in glue and roll them into a point. When this is dry it can act as a 'needle' for threading on the beads (see Fig 13.2).

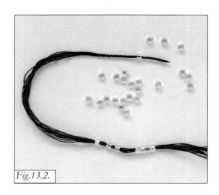

Fig.13.2.

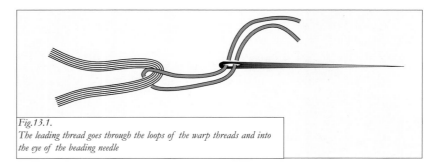

Fig.13.1.
The leading thread goes through the loops of the warp threads and into the eye of the beading needle

SAMPLE 13A

BRAID DETAILS:

Braiding sequence: Round Braid One

Bobbin weight: 70gms (2½oz)

Weight bag: 275gms (10oz)

Finished length: 85cm (33½in)

BEAD DETAILS:

400 'T' - turquoise, silver-lined rocaille
  Bead size: 8/0
1200 'C' - clear, iridescent, silver-lined rocaille
  Bead size: 10/0

WARP DETAILS:

● 16 strands of purple silk, 1.35m (53in) long -
    threaded with 200 x 'C' beads
● 16 strands of turquoise silk, 1.35m (53in) long -
    threaded with 200 x 'T' beads

PREPARATION

The threads are prepared and beaded separately for each bobbin. Take eight lengths of silk 2.7m long and fold them in half. This gives the required sixteen strands of 1.35m for one bobbin. Loops are created at the fold point of the silk strands. Take the leading thread through these loops and thread it into a needle. Now the beads can be added from the needle on to the leading thread and finally on to the silk strands (see Fig 13.1).

When the required number of beads (200) has been added to the silk strands, remove the leading thread.

Repeat this process until all the warp threads have been beaded.

13. EVERY BOBBIN-EVERY SEQUENCE

Temporarily tie the beaded warp threads together by knotting a piece of cotton thread through all of the loops. Make a loop in the tie for the chopstick and S-Hook (see Fig 13.3). Take the warp to the Marudai and attach the beaded threads on to the bobbins.

The beads can sit anywhere on or above the bobbin. However, care will need to be taken to ensure that the slip knot does not snag on the beads.

Fig.13.3

WORKING

Once the weight bag is attached and the bobbins placed in their correct starting positions, then the braiding can commence. The braiding sequence for the round braid is used. Just before each bobbin is moved, push a bead from that bobbin up towards the centre of the Marudai (see Fig 13.4).

Tuck the beads as close to the point of braiding as possible. Continue working, bringing a bead in from every bobbin, every time it is moved.

The instructions read as follows:-

Add a bead from N(right) and S(left).
Make move 1.
Add a bead from E(bottom) and W(top).
Make move 2.

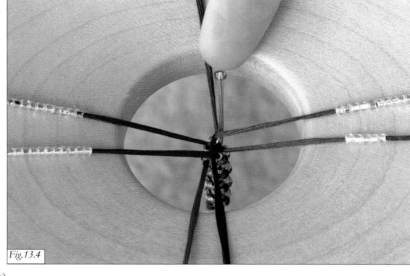

Fig.13.4

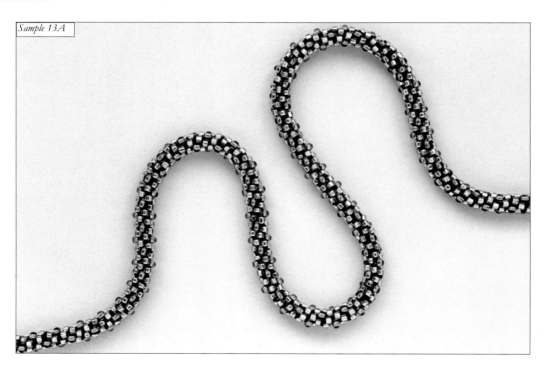

Sample 13A

13. EVERY BOBBIN-EVERY SEQUENCE

SAMPLE 13B

BEAD DETAILS:

920 'F' - frosted, turquoise rocaille
  Bead size: 10/0
920 'P' - purple Delica
  Bead size: 11/0

BRAID DETAILS:

Braiding sequence: Round Braid One

Bobbin weight: 70gms (2½oz)

Weight bag: 275gms (10oz)

Finished length: 85cm (33½in)

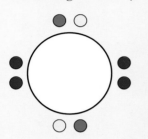

WARP DETAILS:

⬤ 16 strands of purple silk, 1.35m (53in) long -
      threaded with 230 x 'F' beads

◯ 16 strands of lilac silk, 1.35m (53in) long -
      threaded with 230 x 'F' beads

⬤ 16 strands of lilac silk, 1.35m (53in) long -
      threaded with 230 x 'P' beads

WORKING

Prepare a beaded warp using the technique described in Sample 13A but use the warp details shown above.

Work the following instructions:

Add a bead from N(right) and S(left).

Make move 1.

Add a bead from E(bottom) and W(top).

Make move 2.

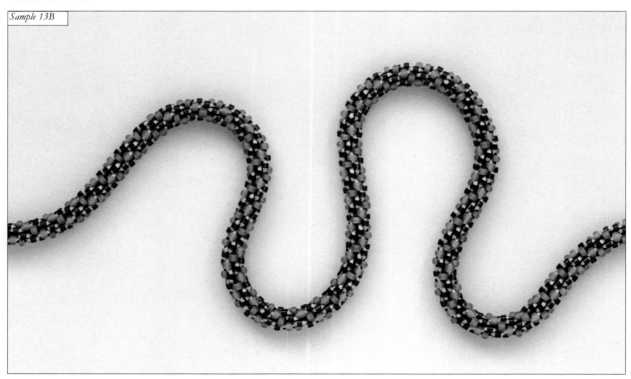

Sample 13B

13. EVERY BOBBIN-EVERY SEQUENCE

SAMPLE 13c

BRAID DETAILS:

Braiding sequence: Round Braid One

Bobbin weight: 70gms (2½oz)

Weight bag: 275gms (10oz)

Finished length: 85cm (33½in)

BEAD DETAILS:

600 'T' - turquoise, silver-lined rocaille
   Bead size: 8/0
1000 'C' - clear, iridescent, silver-lined rocaille
   Bead size: 10/0

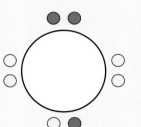

WARP DETAILS:

○ 16 strands of lilac silk, 1.35m (53in) long -
   threaded with 200 x 'C' beads

● 16 strands of turquoise silk, 1.35m (53in) long -
   threaded with 200 x 'T' beads

WORKING

Prepare a beaded warp using the technique described in Sample 13A but use the warp details shown above.

Work the following instructions:

Add a bead from N(right) and S(left).

Make move 1.

Add a bead from E(bottom) and W(top).

Make move 2.

Sample 13C

14 SOME BOBBINS-EVERY SEQUENCE

Here beads are added on to just four of the bobbins. The other four bobbins are wound with plain thread. The beads are added to the threads using the same method as shown in Sample 13A. The method of working is also similar except here the beads are added from some, not all of the bobbins.

SAMPLE 14A

BRAID DETAILS:

Braiding sequence: Spiral Braid One

Bobbin weight: 70gms (2½oz)

Weight bag: 275gms (10oz)

Finished length: 80cm (31½in)

BEAD DETAILS:

640 'G' -iridescent, oily green rocaille
    Bead size: 10/0

WARP DETAILS:

● 14 strands of burgundy silk, 1.35m (53in) long

● 14 strands of green silk, 1.35m (53in) long

● 14 strands of green silk, 1.35m (53in) long - threaded with 160 x 'G' beads

WORKING

Prepare the warp using the details above.
Work repeats of the following instructions:
Add a bead from E(bottom) and W(top).
Make moves 1,2 & 3.

Sample 14A

14. SOME BOBBINS-EVERY SEQUENCE

SAMPLE 14B

BRAID DETAILS:

Braiding sequence: Spiral Braid One

Bobbin weight: 70gms (2½oz)

Weight bag: 275gms (10oz)

Finished length: 80cm (31½in)

BEAD DETAILS:

640 'A' -iridescent, silver-lined amber rocaille
Bead size: 10/0

WARP DETAILS:

● 14 strands of burgundy silk, 1.35m (53in) long

○ 14 strands of cream silk, 1.35m (53in) long -
threaded with 160 x 'A' beads

WORKING: As Sample 14A

Sample 14B

SAMPLE 14C

BRAID DETAILS:

Braiding sequence: Spiral Braid One

Bobbin weight: 70gms (2½oz)

Weight bag: 275gms (10oz)

Finished length: 80cm (31½in)

BEAD DETAILS:

320 'G' -iridescent, oily green rocaille
Bead size: 10/0
320 'A' - iridescent, silver-lined amber rocaille
Bead size: 10/0

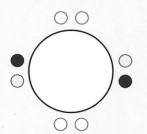

WARP DETAILS:

○ 14 strands of cream silk, 1.35m (53in) long

○ 14 strands of cream silk, 1.35m (53in) long -
threaded with 160 x 'A' beads

● 14 strands of green silk, 1.35m (53in) long -
threaded with 160 x 'G' beads

WORKING: As Sample 14A

Sample 14C

15 SOME BOBBINS-SOME SEQUENCES

These samples take the idea a step further. Beads are added on to some of the bobbins. As the braiding progresses the beads are bought into the braid at particular points within the sequence. Altering where and when beads are introduced to the braid can create different designs.

SAMPLE 15A

BRAID DETAILS:

Braiding sequence: Round Braid Two
Bobbin weight: 70gms (2½oz)
Weight bag: 275gms (10oz)
Finished length: 85cm (33½in)

BEAD DETAILS:

320 'B' - iridescent blue rocaille
    Bead size: 10/0
80 'O' - silver-lined orange rocaille
    Bead size: 10/0

WARP DETAILS:

- ● 16 strands of blue silk, 1.35m (53in) long
- ◐ 16 strands of orange silk, 1.35m (53in) long
- ◯ 16 strands of blue silk, 1.35m (53in) long - threaded with 160 x 'B' beads
- ○ 16 strands of orange silk, 1.35m (53in) long - threaded with 160 x 'O' beads

WORKING

Prepare the warp with beads added to the appropriate threads. The braid sequence is a variation of the Round Braid Two. Work the following instructions:

Make moves 1, 2, 1, 2.
Add a bead from NE and SW.
Make moves 3, 4, 1, 2, 1, 2.
Add a bead from NE, SW and NW.
Make moves 3, 4.

Repeat the whole process until all the beads have been used.

Sample 15A

SAMPLE 15B

BEAD DETAILS:

480 'B' - iridescent blue rocaille
Bead size: 10/0

BRAID DETAILS:

Braiding sequence: Round Braid Two
Bobbin weight: 70gms (2½oz)
Weight bag: 275gms (10oz)
Finished length: 85cm (33½in)

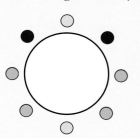

WARP DETAILS:

⬤ 16 strands of orange silk, 1.35m (53in) long

⬤ 16 strands of blue silk, 1.35m (53in) long -
   threaded with 160 x 'B' beads

⬤ 16 strands of blue silk, 1.35m (53in) long -
   threaded with 80 x 'B' beads

WORKING

Prepare and arrange the beaded warp, then work the following:

Make moves 1, 2, 1, 2.
Add a bead from NE and NW.
Make moves 3, 4.
Add a bead from S.
Make moves 1, 2, 1, 2.

Add a bead from SE and SW .
Make moves 3,4.
Add a bead from N.
Repeat the whole sequence.

Sample 15B

15. SOME BOBBINS-SOME SEQUENCES

SAMPLE 15C

BRAID DETAILS:

Braiding sequence: Round Braid Two

Bobbin weight: 70gms (2½oz)

Weight bag: 275gms (10oz)

Finished length: 80cm (31½in)

BEAD DETAILS:

700 'O' - silver-lined orange rocaille
    Bead size: 10/0

50 'G' - round, gold plated metal
    Beads size: 2mm(⁵⁄₆₄in)

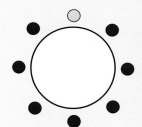

WARP DETAILS:

● 16 strands of blue silk, 1.35m (53in) long -
        threaded with 100 x 'O' beads

◌ 16 strands of blue silk, 1.35m (53in) long -
        threaded with 50 x 'G' beads

WORKING

Work the following instructions taking care to add the beads close to the braid:

Make moves 1, 2.
Add a bead from NE and NW.
Make moves 3, 4.
Add a bead from E and W.
Make moves 1, 2.
Add a bead from SE and SW.
Make moves 3, 4.
Add a bead from S.
Make moves 1, 2.
Add a bead from SE and SW.
Make moves 3, 4.
Add a bead from E and W.
Make moves 1, 2.
Add a bead from NE and NW.
Make moves 3, 4.
Add a bead from N.

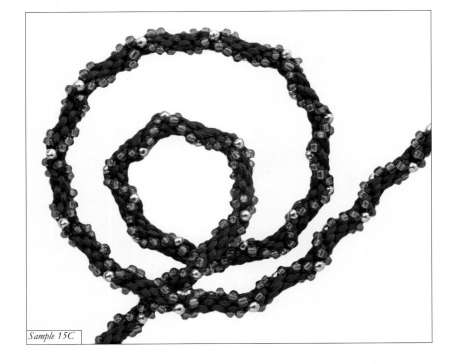

Sample 15C

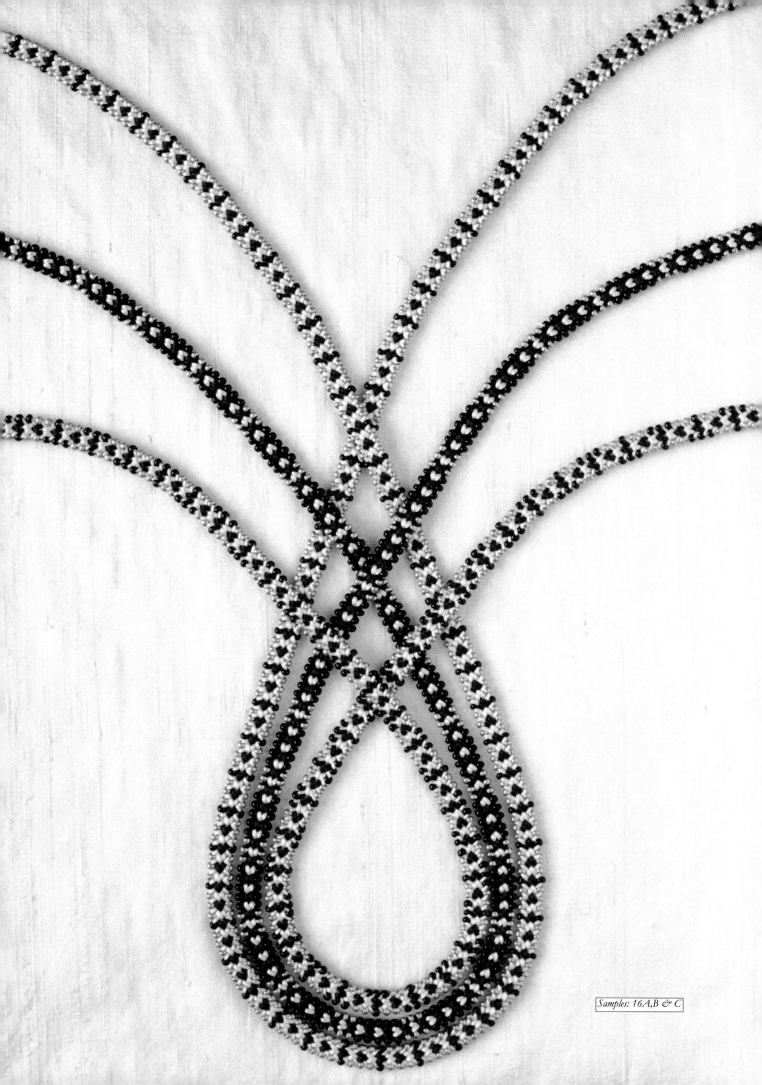

Samples: 16A,B & C

16 COLOUR ORDER

These samples also have beads added to the warp before braiding begins. (Don't forget that preparing this type of warp is discussed on page 72). Here, different coloured beads are added on to the same threads. When these are worked, the order in which the colours appear creates different designs on the braid. It is therefore very important to prepare the colours correctly because one error will throw the whole pattern out of sequence. When preparing the warp make sure that the bead closest to the centre of the Marudai is the first one described in the colour order sequence. The samples are worked by positioning the beads on the edges of Flat Braid One. Take care to push the beads as close to the braid as possible and re-adjust if necessary.

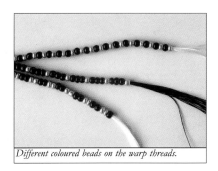

Different coloured beads on the warp threads.

SAMPLE 16A

BEAD DETAILS:

160 'B' - black rocaille
    Bead size: 10/0
480 'G' - gold metallic rocaille
    Bead size: 10/0

BRAID DETAILS:

Braiding sequence: Flat Braid One
Bobbin weight: 70gms (2½oz)
Weight bag: 275gms (10oz)
Finished length: 85cm (33½in)

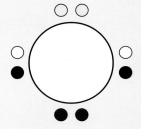

WARP DETAILS:

○ 16 strands of cream Biron, 1.35m (53in) long
● 16 strands of navy Biron, 1.35m (53in) long
○ 16 strands of cream Biron, 1.35m (53in) long -
    threaded with 160 x 'BG' beads
● 16 strands of cream Biron, 1.35m (53in) long -
    threaded with 160 beads in colour order 'G'

WORKING

Work repeats of the following instructions:
Make moves 1, 2, 3 & 4.
Add a bead from E(bottom) and W(bottom).

The beads will appear in the braid in matching pairs of colour.
The first beads to appear should be black, followed by three pairs of gold beads.

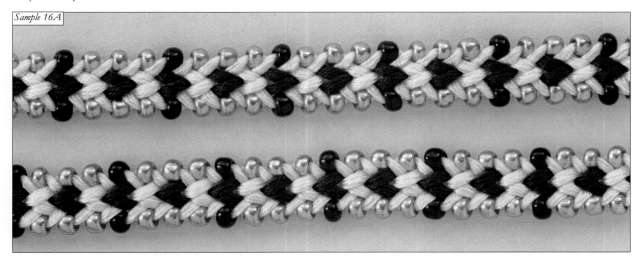

Sample 16A

16. COLOUR ORDER

SAMPLE 16B

BRAID DETAILS:

Braiding sequence: Flat Braid One
Bobbin weight: 70gms (2½oz)
Weight bag: 275gms (10oz)
Finished length: 85cm (33½in)

BEAD DETAILS:

400 'B' - black rocaille
    Bead size: 10/0
240 'G' - gold metallic rocaille
    Bead size: 10/0

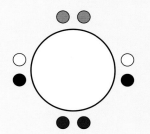

WARP DETAILS:

○ 16 strands of cream Biron, 1.35m (53in) long
● 16 strands of navy Biron, 1.35m (53in) long
● 16 strands of black Biron, 1.35m (53in) long -
    threaded with 160 beads in colour order 'BBBG'
● 16 strands of black Biron, 1.35m (53in) long -
    threaded with 160 beads in colour order 'BBGG'

WORKING Same as Sample 16A

Sample 16B

SAMPLE 16C

BRAID DETAILS:

Braiding sequence: Flat Braid One
Bobbin weight: 70gms (2½oz)
Weight bag: 275gms (10oz)
Finished length: 85cm (33½in)

BEAD DETAILS:
240 'B' - black rocaille
    Bead size: 10/0
320 'G' - gold metallic rocaille
    Bead size: 10/0
80 'N' - navy rocaille
    Bead size: 8/0

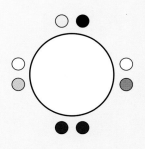

WARP DETAILS:
○ 16 strands of cream Biron, 1.35m (53in) long.
● 16 strands of navy Biron, 1.35m (53in) long
○ 16 strands of cream Biron, 1.35m (53in) long -
    threaded with 160 beads in colour order 'BGGB'
● 16 strands of cream Biron, 1.35m (53in) long -
    threaded with 160 beads in colour order 'GBBG'
● 16 strands of cream Biron, 1.35m (53in) long -
    threaded with 160 beads in colour order 'NGBG'
○ 16 strands of cream Biron, 1.35m (53in) long -
    threaded with 160 beads in colour order 'BGNG'

WORKING Same as Sample 16A

Sample 16C

17 CLUSTERS

The samples so far have involved pushing just one bead at a time into the braid. However, adding several beads at a time can form clusters. A variation of Round Braid Two produces elongated stitches. These are perfectly suited to accommodate several beads allowing them to sit comfortably in the braid structure.

SAMPLE 17A

BEAD DETAILS:

360 'B' - blue iridescent rocaille
    Bead size: 10/0
1080 'L' - light blue iridescent rocaille
    Bead size: 8/0

BRAID DETAILS:

Braiding sequence: Round Braid Two
Bobbin weight: 70gms (2½oz)
Weight bag: 275gms (10oz)
Finished length: 90cm (35in)

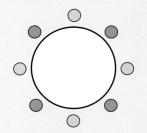

WARP DETAILS:

⚪ 16 strands of mauve Biron, 1.35m (53in) long -
    threaded with 90 x 'B' beads
⚫ 16 strands of grey Biron, 1.35m (53in) long -
    threaded with 270 x 'L' beads

WORKING

Prepare a beaded warp using the details shown.
(The method is still the one discussed on page 72).
Work the following repeated instructions:

Make moves 1,2,1,2,1,2.
Add three beads from NE, NW, SE and SW.
Make moves 3,4,3,4.
Add one bead from N, S, E and W.

Sample 17A

SAMPLE 17B

BRAID DETAILS:

Braiding sequence: Round Braid Two

Bobbin weight: 70gms (2½oz)

Weight bag: 275gms (10oz)

Finished length: 95cm (37in)

BEAD DETAILS:

1056 'P' - purple frosted rocaille
    Bead size: 8/0
1056 'L' - light blue iridescent rocaille
    Bead size: 8/0

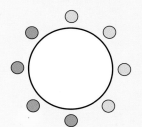

WARP DETAILS:

○ 16 strands of mauve Biron, 1.35m (53in) long - threaded with 264 x 'P' beads

● 16 strands of grey Biron, 1.35m (53in) long - threaded with 264 x 'L' beads

WORKING

Work the following instructions:

*Make moves 1,2,1,2,1,2.

Add three beads from NE, NW, SE and SW.

Make moves 3,4,3,4,3,4.

Add three beads from N, S, E and W.

Repeat from * until eleven clusters have been created.

(The eleventh cluster is created by working just the first half of the sequence.)

Now work twelve repeats of Round Braid Two before starting the whole process again.

Sample 17B

SAMPLE 17C

BRAID DETAILS:

Braiding sequence: Round Braid Two

Bobbin weight: 70gms (2½oz)

Weight bag: 275gms (10oz)

Finished length: 95cm (37in)

BEAD DETAILS:

1056 'P' - purple frosted rocaille
Bead size: 8/0
1056 'L' - light blue iridescent rocaille
Bead size: 8/0

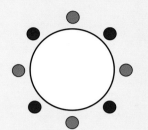

WARP DETAILS:

● 16 strands of purple Biron, 1.35m (53in) long - threaded with 264 x 'P' beads

● 16 strands of blue Biron, 1.35m (53in) long - threaded with 264 x 'L' beads

WORKING

*Make moves 1,2,1,2,1,2.

Add three beads from NW, NE, SW and SE.

Make moves 3,4,3,4,3,4.

Add three beads from N, S, E and W.

Repeat from * until eleven clusters have been created.

(the eleventh one is made by working just the first half of the sequence).

Then work eight repeats of moves 1,2,1,2,3,4 before starting the whole process again.

Sample 17C

18 RANDOM

These samples continue with the idea of adding beads on to the warp threads during preparation. However, the beads are pushed into the braiding work in a random manner, creating a scattering of beads. In these samples they lie on the outer edge of the spiral braid.

SAMPLE 18A

BRAID DETAILS:

Braiding sequence: Spiral Braid Two

Bobbin weight: 70gms (2½oz)

Weight bag: 275gms (10oz)

Finished length: 70cm (27½in)

BEAD DETAILS:

640 'B' - burgundy rocaille
   Bead size: 11/0
80 'L' - lilac rocaille
   Bead size: 10/0

WARP DETAILS:

- 16 strands of burgundy silk, 1.35m (53in) long
- 16 strands of grey silk, 1.35m (53in) long - threaded with 160 x 'B' beads
- 16 strands of grey silk, 1.35m (53in) long - threaded with 40 x 'L' beads

WORKING

Add beads from any bobbin in a random manner whilst working Spiral Braid Two.

Sample 18A

---
18. RANDOM

SAMPLE 18B

BEAD DETAILS:

320 'G' - gun metal rocaille
Bead size: 10/0

BRAID DETAILS:

Braiding sequence: Spiral Braid Two

Bobbin weight: 70gms (2½oz)

Weight bag: 275gms (10oz)

Finished length: 70cm (27½in)

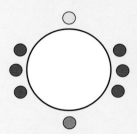

WARP DETAILS:

○ 16 strands of pale pink silk, 1.35m (53in) long

● 16 strands of grey silk, 1.35m (53in) long

● 16 strands of burgundy silk, 1.35m (53in) long
  threaded with 60 x 'G' beads

WORKING: Same as Sample 18A

Sample 18B

SAMPLE 18C

BEAD DETAILS:

360 ' C' clear iridescent rocaille
Bead size: 10/0

BRAID DETAILS:

Braiding sequence: Spiral Braid Two

Bobbin weight: 70gms (2½oz)

Weight bag: 275gms (10oz)

Finished length: 70cm (27½in)

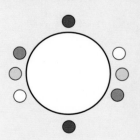

WARP DETAILS:

● 16 strands of burgundy silk, 1.35m (53in) long

● 16 strands of grey silk, 1.35m (53in) long -
  threaded with 60 x 'C' beads

○ 16 strands of pale pink silk, 1.35m (53in) long -
  threaded with 60 x 'C' beads

○ 16 strands of white silk, 1.35m (53in) long -
  threaded with 60 x 'C' beads

WORKING: Same as Sample 18A

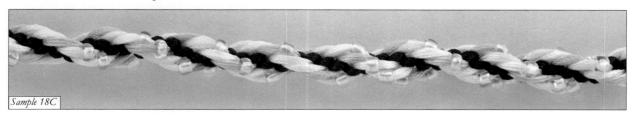

Sample 18C

19 THICK & THIN

One of the disadvantages of putting beads directly on to the warp threads is that the braids can seem very thin in comparison to the bead size. This is because the size of the bead hole dictates the amount of thread that can go through it.

One solution to this dilemma is to add extra threads on to the bobbins that do not require beading. The braid will be distorted because there are different quantities of thread being used but the overall effect will be a greater volume of braid. Use 100gm bobbins for the large quantity of threads and 70gm ones for the others.

SAMPLE 19A

BRAID DETAILS:

Braiding sequence: Flat Braid One

Bobbin weight: 100&70gms (3½&2½oz)

Weight bag: 325gms (10oz)

Finished length: 80cm (31½in)

BEAD DETAILS:

180 'B' iridescent oily blue rocaille
    Bead size: 10/0
180 'R' iridescent oily red rocaille
    Bead size: 10/0

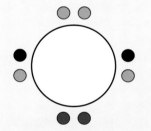

WARP DETAILS:

● 80 strands of rust Biron, 1.35m (53in) long

● 16 strands of burgundy Biron, 1.35m (53in) long -
    threaded with 90 x 'B' beads

● 16 strands of burgundy Biron, 1.35m (53in) long -
    threaded with 90 x 'R' beads

WORKING

Prepare the warp as detailed.
Work the following instructions:
Make moves 1, 2, 3, 4.
Add a bead from S(left) and S(right).

Sample 19A

19. THICK & THIN

SAMPLE 19B

BRAID DETAILS:

Braiding sequence: Flat Braid One

Bobbin weight: 100&70gms (3½&2½oz)

Weight bag: 325gms (10oz)

Finished length: 80cm (31½in)

BEAD DETAILS:

180 'B' iridescent oily blue rocaille
Bead size: 10/0

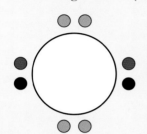

WARP DETAILS:

● 80 strands of rust Biron, 1.35m (53in) long

● 16 strands of burgundy Biron, 1.35m (53in) long

● 16 strands of burgundy Biron, 1.35m (53in) long -
threaded with 90 x 'B' beads

WORKING

Make moves 1, 2, 3, 4, 1, 2, 3, 4.

Add a bead from E(bottom) and W(bottom).

Sample 19B

SAMPLE 19C

BRAID DETAILS:

Braiding sequence: Flat Braid One

Bobbin weight: 100&70gms (3½&2½oz)

Weight bag: 325gms (10oz)

Finished length: 80cm (31½in)

BEAD DETAILS:

180 'B' iridescent oily blue rocaille
    Bead size: 10/0

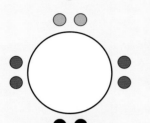

WARP DETAILS:

- 80 strands of burgundy Biron, 1.35m (53in) long
- 16 strands of rust Biron, 1.35m (53in) long
- 16 strands of rust Biron, 1.35m (53in) long - threaded with 90 x 'B' beads

WORKING

Make moves 1, 2, 3, 4, 1, 2, 3, 4.
Add a bead from S(left) and S(right).

Sample 19C

20 SOME THREADS

Another way of adding to the volume of beaded braids is by putting lots of thread on each bobbin. Although the beads will not fit over all of these threads, they can be threaded on to as many as possible (see Fig 20.1). Beads that do not sit on all of the threads can look rather imprecise. This is due to the fact that the beads can sit on the outer edge of the stitches or be hidden beneath threads in the interior of the braid. It is possible to control the position of the beads but these samples allow the random nature of this method to take the lead, creating a scattered bead effect. However, an effort has been made to ensure that the beads are added below the point of braiding.

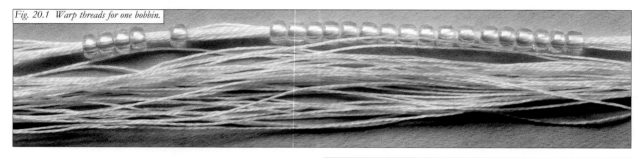

Fig. 20.1 Warp threads for one bobbin.

SAMPLE 20A

BRAID DETAILS:

Braiding sequence: Spiral Braid Two

Bobbin weight: 100gms (3½oz)

Weight bag: 375gms (13oz)

Finished length: 70cm (27½in)

BEAD DETAILS:

2400 'C' - cream rocaille
Bead size: 10/0

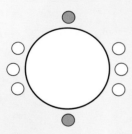

WARP DETAILS:

- ● 40 strands of rust Biron, 1.35m (53in) long
- ○ 48 strands of cream Biron, 1.35m (53in) long - with 8 strands threaded with 400 x 'C' beads

WORKING

Make moves 1, 2.
Add five beads from E(bottom) and W(top).

Sample 20A

SAMPLE 20B

BRAID DETAILS:

Braiding sequence: Spiral Braid Two

Bobbin weight: 100gms (3½oz)

Weight bag: 375gms (13oz)

Finished length: 70cm (27½in)

BEAD DETAILS:

1200 'M' - mix of orange and metallic rocaille
Bead size: 10/0

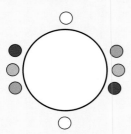

WARP DETAILS:

○ 40 strands of cream Biron, 1.35m (53in) long

◔ 48 strands of rust Biron, 1.35m (53in) long -
with 8 strands threaded with 200 x 'M' beads

◔ 48 strands of tan Biron, 1.35m (53in) long -
with 8 strands threaded with 200 x 'M' beads

● 48 strands of brown Biron, 1.35m (53in) long
with 8 strands threaded with 200 x 'M' beads

WORKING:

As Sample 20A except the beads are added after every other sequence of moves.

Sample 20B

SAMPLE 20C

BRAID DETAILS:

Braiding sequence: Spiral Braid Two

Bobbin weight: 100gms (3½oz)

Weight bag: 375gms (13oz)

Finished length: 70cm (27½in)

BEAD DETAILS:

600 'O' - orange silver-lined rocaille
Bead size: 10/0

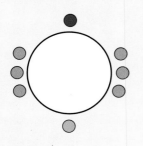

WARP DETAILS:

● 40 strands of brown Biron, 1.35m (53in) long

◔ 40 strands of tan Biron, 1.35m (53in) long

◔ 48 strands of rust Biron, 1.35m (53in) long -
with 8 strands threaded with 100 x 'O' beads

WORKING

Add beads randomly from the bobbins in position E(bottom) and W(top).

Sample 20C

21 DIFFERENT BEADS

So far in this chapter we have just looked at using rocaille beads. When different types of beads are added to the warp, the effects can be quite stunning.

However, larger beads do need space to sit within the braid structure. The variation of Round Braid Two creates large, floating threads that can accom- modate these beads. The addi- tion of rocaille beads also help to space the larger beads into the braid structure.

SAMPLE 21A

BRAID DETAILS:

Braiding sequence: Round Braid Two

Bobbin weight: 70gms (2½oz)

Weight bag: 275gms (10oz)

Finished length: 80cm (31½in)

BEAD DETAILS:

200 'Y' - yellow silver-lined bugle
    Bead size:4mm(⁵⁄₃₂in) long
100 'G' - gold plated metal
    Bead size: 2mm(⁵⁄₆₄in)

WARP DETAILS:

- ● 20 strands of blue Biron, 1.35m (53in) long
- ● 20 strands of purple Biron, 1.35m (53in) long
- ● 12 strands of green Biron, 1.35m (53in) long - threaded with 25 groups of 'YGY' beads

WORKING

Prepare the warp using the details shown and then work the following instructions:

Make moves 1,2,1,2,1,2,1,2.

Add three beads (bugle, gold, bugle) from NE, NW, SE and SW.

Make moves 3, 4.

Make four repeats of the moves 1,2,1,2,3,4.

Sample 21A

21. DIFFERENT BEADS

SAMPLE 21B

BRAID DETAILS:

Braiding sequence: Round Braid Two

Bobbin weight: 70gms (2½oz)

Weight bag: 275gms (10oz)

Finished length: 80cm (31½in)

BEAD DETAILS:

96 'R' - gold coloured plastic rosettes
   Bead size: 6x3mm (¼ x⅛in)

384 'G' - gold plated metal
   Bead size: 2mm(⁵⁄₆₄in)

WARP DETAILS:

- 20 strands of blue Biron, 1.35m (53in) long
- 20 strands of purple Biron, 1.35m (53in) long
- 14 strands of green Biron, 1.35m (53in) long - threaded with 24 groups of 'GGRGG' beads

WORKING

 *Make five repeats of moves 1 and 2.

Add five beads (two gold, a rosette and two gold) from NE, NW, SE and SW.

Make moves 3,4,1,2,1,2,3,4. Repeat from * two more times.

Then make seven sequences of moves 1,2,1,2,3,4 to create the space between the groups of three clusters.

Repeat the whole series of instructions until all the beads have been used.

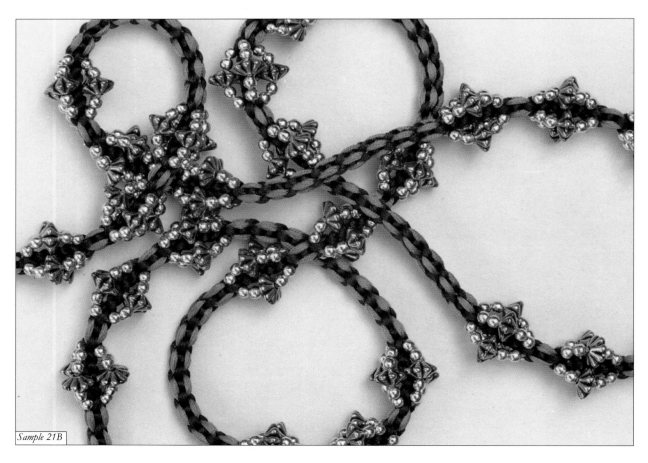

Sample 21B

SAMPLE 21C

BRAID DETAILS:

Braiding sequence: Round Braid Two

Bobbin weight: 70gms (2½oz)

Weight bag: 275gms (10oz)

Finished length: 70cm (27½in)

BEAD DETAILS:

275 'B' - black rocaille
   Bead size:10/0

55 'D' - black drop
   Bead size:15x6mm(⅝x¼in)

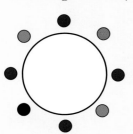

WARP DETAILS:

- 20 strands of blue Biron, 1.35m (53in) long
- 14 strands of green Biron, 1.35m (53in) long
- 14 strands of green Biron, 1.35m (53in) long - threaded with 55 x 'B' beads
- 14 strands of green Biron, 1.35m (53in) long - threaded with 55 groups of 'BBDBB' beads

WORKING

Make moves 1,2,1,2,1,2.

Add one bead from NE and five beads (two rocailles, drop bead, two rocailles) SW.

Make moves 3,4,1,2,3,4.

Note that the cluster of beads will tend to travel over the point of braiding and may need re-adjusting so that they sit on a curve away from the edge of the braid.

Sample 21C

22 STRINGS

Instead of thread, strings of rocaille beads can be used to make a warp. Although this may seem straightforward, the tensioning can be tricky. The action of braiding pushes the beads apart. This forces the beads up along the string and gradually builds up the pressure. If this is not smoothly released at frequent intervals, changes in the make up of the braid will occur. If the beads are too loose on the string, the braiding looks sparse and bits of the beading thread can show through. However, if the beads become too tight, the braid becomes stiffer and more lattice-like in its appearance. At worst, the pressure can become so great that it causes the beading thread to snap.

To make the strings of beads, take a length of beading thread 1m (39in) long. Use a needle to thread on one bead. Take the needle over the bead and back through the inside. This is your stopper bead (see Fig 22.1).

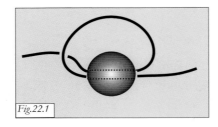

Fig.22.1

It prevents the other beads from moving along the beading thread. It is not very firm so care must be taken whilst preparing the warp. However, this is an advantage because the bead can be slid along the thread when necessary to release the tension whilst braiding. When the stopper bead is in position near the end of the thread, add more beads to the string. Continue adding beads until they cover 70cm (28in) of the thread. The rest of the uncovered thread will be used when releasing the tension during braiding.

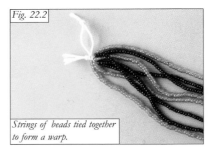

Fig. 22.2

Strings of beads tied together to form a warp.

SAMPLE 22A

BEAD DETAILS:

4 strings of blue colour-lined rocaille
    Bead size: 10/0 String length: 70cm(27½in)
4 strings of iridescent oily blue rocaille
    Bead size: 10/0 String length: 70cm(27½in)

BRAID DETAILS:

Braiding sequence: Square Braid
Bobbin weight: 70gms (2½oz)
Weight bag: 275gms (10oz)
Finished length: 55cm (22in)

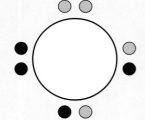

WARP DETAILS:

○ 1 string of blue beads, 70cm (27½in) long
● 1 string of oily blue beads, 70cm (27½in) long

WORKING

Prepare eight strings of beads as detailed above. Tightly tie all eight strings together at the top end furthest from the stopper bead and add a loop in the tie for the chopstick and S-hook (see Fig 22.2). Bring the 'warp' of beads to the Marudai and add the bobbins in the usual manner.

Arrange the strings of beads in their correct starting positions making sure that the beads are pushed up to the point of braiding. All the spare beading thread will be closest to the bobbin.

Use the sequence of moves to produce the square braid. Frequently stop braiding and ease the beads along the thread by moving the stopper bead. Try to do this little and often to keep

22. STRINGS

the pressure constant. Try to finish the strings at the same time, to give a clean end to the piece. However, if the take up has been uneven, push any surplus beads up along the thread so that the braid can end with a small section of braided thread. This can be knotted or whipped to secure the braid.

Sample 22A in progress.

Sample 22A

SAMPLE 22B

BRAID DETAILS:

Braiding sequence: Square Braid

Bobbin weight: 70gms (2½oz)

Weight bag: 275gms (10oz)

Finished length: 55cm (22in)

BEAD DETAILS:

2 strings of red rocaille.
   Bead size: 10/0 String length: 70cm(27½in)

2 strings of orange silver-lined rocaille
   Bead size: 10/0 String length: 70cm(27½in)

2 strings of yellow silver-lined rocaille
   Bead size: 10/0 String length: 70cm(27½in)

2 strings of cream silver-lined rocaille
   Bead size: 10/0 String length: 70cm(27½in)

WARP DETAILS:

1 string of red beads, 70cm (27½in) long

1 string of orange beads, 70cm (27½in) long

1 string of yellow beads, 70cm (27½in) long

1 string of cream beads, 70cm (27½in) long

WORKING: As Sample 22A.

Sample 22B

SAMPLE 22C

BRAID DETAILS:

Braiding sequence: Square Braid

Bobbin weight: 70gms (2½oz)

Weight bag: 275gms (10oz)

Finished length: 55cm (22in)

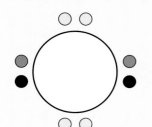

BEAD DETAILS:

4 strings of pale green colour-lined rocaille
    Bead size: 10/0 String length: 70cm(27½in)

2 strings of green rocaille
    Bead size: 10/0 String length: 70cm(27½in)

2 strings of dark green rocaille
    Bead size: 10/0 String length: 70cm(27½in)

WARP DETAILS:

○ 1 string of pale green beads, 70cm (27½in) long

◐ 1 string of green beads, 70cm (27½in) long

● 1 string of dark green beads, 70cm (27½in) long

WORKING: As Sample 22A.

Sample 22C

23 MIXED STRINGS

The finished appearance of a braid is dependent on the type and size of the warp threads used to produce it. This also applies to warps made with strings of beads. These examples are worked with combinations of different bead sizes and types. Note that the problems with tension discussed on page 98 still apply.

SAMPLE 23A

BRAID DETAILS:

Braiding sequence: Round Braid One

Bobbin weight: 70gms (2½oz)

Weight bag: 275gms (10oz)

Finished length: 45cm (18in)

BEAD DETAILS:

6 strings of pearl rocaille
  Bead size: 10/0 String length: 70cm(27½in)
2 strings of semi-precious Citrine tumblestones
  Bead size: 3mm(⅛in) String length: 70cm(27½in)

WARP DETAILS:

○ 1 string of pearl beads, 70cm(27½in) long
◉ 1 string of Citrine beads, 70cm(27½in) long

WORKING

Prepare the strings of beads in the same manner as Sample 22A. Use the sequence of moves for Round Braid One to produce the braid.

Sample 23A

SAMPLE 23B

BRAID DETAILS:

Braiding sequence: Round Braid One

Bobbin weight: 70gms (2½oz)

Weight bag: 275gms (10oz)

Finished length: 55cm (22in)

BEAD DETAILS:

4 strings of pearl rocaille
    Bead size: 10/0 String length: 70cm(27½in)
4 strings of bronze metallic hexagonal rocaille
    Bead size: 8/0 String length: 70cm(27½in)

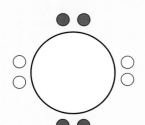

WARP DETAILS:

○ 1 string of pearl beads, 70cm(27½in) long

● 1 string of bronze beads, 70cm(27½in) long

WORKING: Same as Sample 23A

Sample 23B

SAMPLE 23C

BRAID DETAILS:

Braiding sequence: Round Braid One

Bobbin weight: 70gms (2½oz)

Weight bag: 275gms (10oz)

Finished length: 45cm (18in)

BEAD DETAILS:

4 strings of pearl rocaille
    Bead size: 10/0 String length: 70cm(27½in)
4 strings of alternate amber rocaille (10/0) and
    4mm(⁵⁄₃₂in) cream beads
    String length: 70cm(27½in)

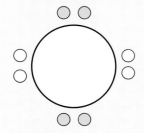

WARP DETAILS:

○ 1 string of pearl beads, 70cm(27½in) long

◐ 1 string of alternate beads, 70cm(27½in) long

WORKING: Same as Sample 23A

Sample 23C

24 STRINGS & THREAD

Here is another variation of using strings of beads that are prepared using the technique discussed on page 98 This time only some of the warp is made from strings. The rest consists of threads. Both sections of the warp (strings and thread) are tied together at the start and then prepared in the normal manner.

SAMPLE 24A

BRAID DETAILS:

Braiding sequence: Spiral Braid One
Bobbin weight: 100gms (3½oz)
Weight bag: 375gms (10oz)
Finished length: 70cm (27½in)

BEAD DETAILS:

2 strings of yellow silver-lined rocaille
    Bead size: 10/0 String length: 110cm(43in)

WARP DETAILS:

● 40 strands of red Biron, 1.35m (53in) long
● 40 strands of brown Biron, 1.35m (53in) long
○ 1 string of yellow beads, 110cm (43in) long

WORKING

Work the sequence of moves for Spiral Braid One with the warp made using the instructions above.

Sample 24A

24. STRINGS & THREAD

SAMPLE 24B

BRAID DETAILS:

Braiding sequence: Spiral Braid One

Bobbin weight: 100gms (3½oz)

Weight bag: 375gms (10oz)

Finished length: 70cm (27½in)

BEAD DETAILS:

4 strings of yellow silver-lined rocaille
  Bead size: 10/0 String length: 110cm(43in)

WARP DETAILS:

- ● 40 strands of red Biron, 1.35m (53in) long
- ● 40 strands of brown Biron, 1.35m (53in) long
- ○ 1 string of yellow beads, 110cm (43in) long

WORKING Same as Sample 24A

Sample 24B

SAMPLE 24C

BRAID DETAILS:

Braiding sequence: Spiral Braid One

Bobbin weight: 100gms (3½oz)

Weight bag: 375gms (10oz)

Finished length: 70cm (27½in)

BEAD DETAILS:

4 strings of alternate yellow and red rocaille
  Bead size: 10/0 String length: 110cm(43in)

WARP DETAILS:

- ● 40 strands of brown Biron, 1.35m (53in) long
- ○ 1 string of alternate beads, 110cm (43in) long

WORKING Same as Sample 24A

Sample 24C

25 DIRECT ATTACHMENT

This method gives a direct join between beads and braids but it is only suitable for certain types of bead. The hole of the bead needs to be large enough for the warp threads to be knotted through. The position of the hole is also important as it effects how the bead hangs from the braid.

The warp threads are initially prepared to give half the quantity but twice the length of the final requirements. When the threads are folded in half the correct warp details are produced. This makes loops of thread at the (half way) fold point. These loops are taken

through the bead hole and back over the ends to form a Lark's head knot. Two braids are made in succession and both attach directly on to the bead so that the final result has the bead hanging at the centre of the two braids.

SAMPLE 25A

BRAID DETAILS:

Braiding sequence: Rectangular Braid

Bobbin weight: 100gms (3½oz)

Weight bag: 375gms (13oz)

Finished length: 75cm (29½in)

WARP DETAILS:

● 40 strands of black Biron, 67cm (26in) long

● 40 strands of green Biron, 67cm (26in) long

BEAD DETAILS:

1 hematine ring
Bead size: 23mm (²⁹⁄₃₂in) Hole size:19mm (¾in)

WORKING

Take a half rope length (full rope thickness) of black Biron and fold it in half. This gives you the thread for two bobbins. Use a Lark's head knot to attach the threads on to the ring. This is shown as the knot furthest left in Fig. 25.1

Now add the green threads in the same way so that the Lark's head knots sit next to each other. Finally add another half rope of black (see Fig. 25.1). It is worth spending time stroking out the threads and getting them to lie neatly over the ring.

Tie a small loop of spare cotton on to the ring (see Fig.25.2). This loop is for attaching the chopstick (and later the S-hook)

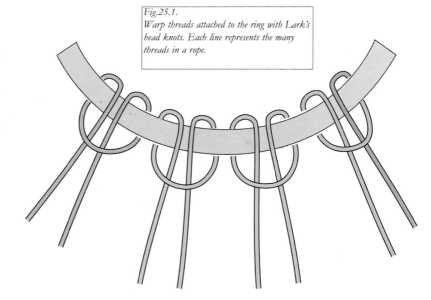

Fig.25.1.
Warp threads attached to the ring with Lark's head knots. Each line represents the many threads in a rope.

25. DIRECT ATTACHMENT

although in this sample it is possible to use the ring directly.

Now the warp can be brought to the Marudai and attached to the bobbins. The ring will hang directly below the starting point of the braid. Arrange the position of the colours and commence braiding. Take time to make the arrangement and first stitches as neat as possible to get the best results.

Finish the first braid, and then repeat the whole process with another warp on the other side of the ring (see Fig. 25.3).

Fig. 25.2.
The first warp attached to the ring.

Fig. 25.3.
When the first warp has been completed, the second warp can be attached to the ring.

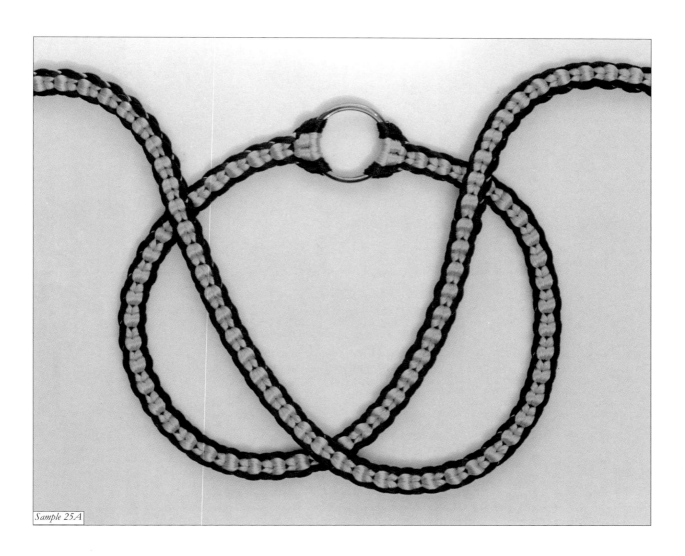

Sample 25A

25. DIRECT ATTACHMENT

SAMPLE 25B

BRAID DETAILS:

Braiding sequence: Rectangular Braid

Bobbin weight: 70gms (2½oz)

Weight bag: 275gms (10oz)

Finished length: 75cm (29½in)

BEAD DETAILS:

1 hematine oval pendant

Bead size: 35x25mm(1⅜x1in)

Hole size: 16x12mm(⅝x¹⁵⁄₃₂in)

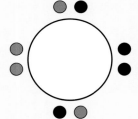

WARP DETAILS:

● 20 strands of black Biron, 67cm (26in) long

● 20 strands of green Biron, 67cm (26in) long

WORKING

The same idea is used to attach the pendant bead. However, this time the warp is added with just two knots (see Fig 25.4). Add all the green threads for the first warp on to the pendant, then add all of the black threads. Complete the first braid before attaching the second warp on to the pendant.

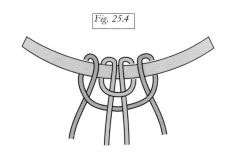

Fig. 25.4

Sample 25B

25. DIRECT ATTACHMENT

SAMPLE 25C

BRAID DETAILS:

Braiding sequence: Rectangular Braid

Bobbin weight: 70gms (2½oz)

Weight bag: 275gms (10oz)

Finished length: 75cm (29½in)

BEAD DETAILS:

1 hematine heart
   Bead size: 30x38mm(1³⁄₁₆x1½in)
   Hole size: 12mm(¹⁵⁄₃₂in)

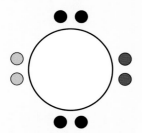

WARP DETAILS:

● 20 strands of black Biron, 67cm (26in) long

◔ 20 strands of green Biron, 67cm (26in) long

◕ 20 strands of dark green Biron, 67cm (26in) long

WORKING

This time all the threads for both of the braids are knotted on to the pendant at the same time (see Fig 25.5). Add all of the light green threads first, and then the dark green ones and finally the black threads over the top of them all. Divide the threads into two groups. Use one group to wind on to the bobbins to produce the first braid. Let the other group of threads hang below the heart bead under the mirror. After the first braid is finished, use the other group to re-wind the bobbins to make the second braid.

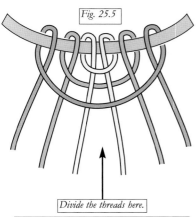

Fig. 25.5

Divide the threads here.

The threads to the left are for the first warp and the threads to the right are for the second warp.

Sample 25C

GALLERY 13

Necklace made from combining large
Lampwork beads with a beaded braid.
The small beads were added from
every bobbin, every sequence.

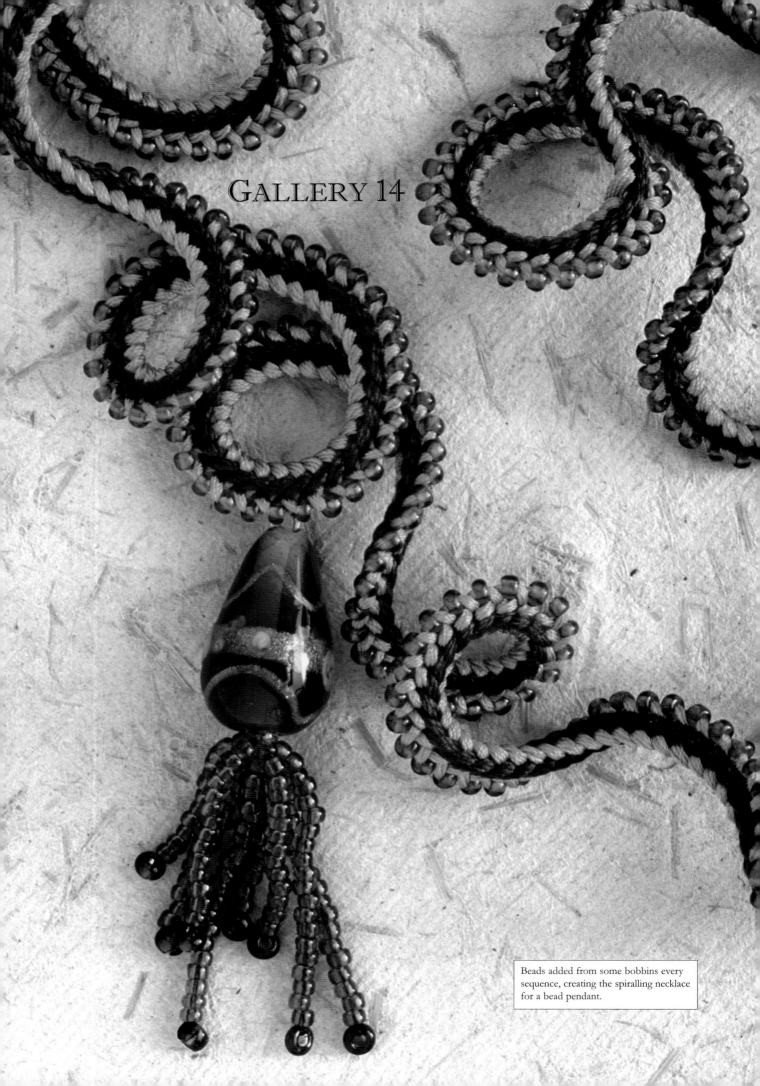

GALLERY 14

Beads added from some bobbins every
sequence, creating the spiralling necklace
for a bead pendant.

Oily Rocaille beads are added at specific points in the braiding process so that they sit comfortably within the honey-comb structure of this silk necklace.

A series of coloured beads produce the design for this Indian bell necklace.

A range of designs using beads added in clusters.

Detail of braid made from fishing line randomly incorporting Rose Quartz and Garnet beads.

Samples of braids made using 'Thick and Thin' warp threads.

Tiny pearly beads are threaded in amongst the textured warp threads.

Necklace made from a silk braid
and different shaped beads
including Malachite drops.

A Venetian bead hanging from a braid
made from strings of rocaille beads.

Necklace created from strings of different beads.

GALLERY 24

Pin brooch made from a swirl of silk threads and strung Malachite beads.

The silk warp threads were directly attached to the 'Urn' bead at the start of the braiding process.

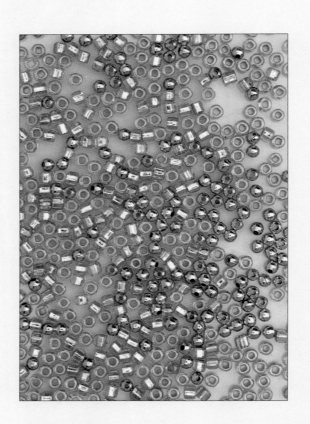

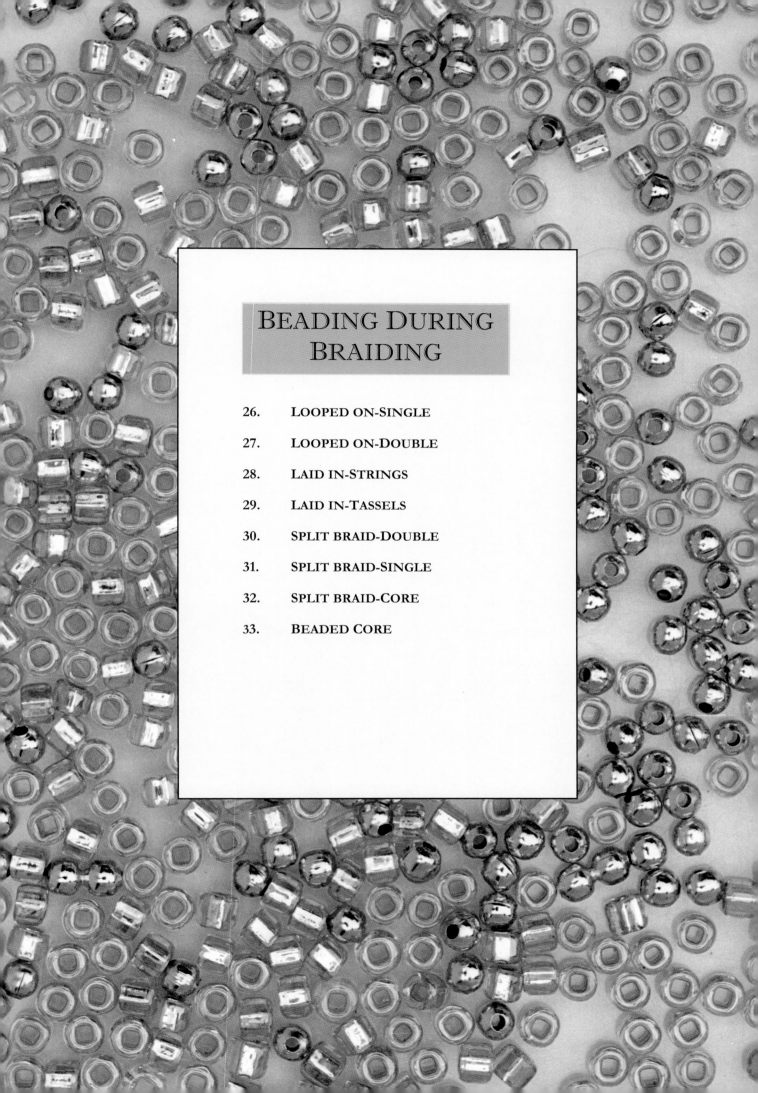

BEADING DURING BRAIDING

26 LOOPED ON-SINGLE

Consideration needs to be given to the size of the bead hole as the bead is attached by taking a loop of warp threads through the beads. A crochet hook can be a useful tool for getting the threads through the bead. Another alternative is to take a piece of spare cotton over the threads. Take both ends of the cotton through the bead hole and use it to pull a loop of threads through (see Fig 26.1).

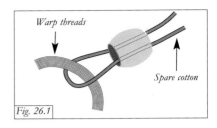

Warp threads

Spare cotton

Fig. 26.1

SAMPLE 26A

BRAID DETAILS:

Braiding sequence: Spiral Braid One

Bobbin weight: 70gms (2½oz)

Weight bag: 275gms (10oz)

Finished length: 80cm (31in)

BEAD DETAILS:

1 gold coloured metal pendant
    Bead size: 43x10mm(1⅔x¹³⁄₃₂in)
    Hole size: 3mm(⅛in)

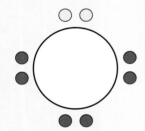

WARP DETAILS:

● 20 strands of red Biron, 1.35m (53in) long
○ 15 strands of gold metallised Biron, 1.35m (53in) long

WORKING

Prepare a warp using the details shown and start braiding. The pendant bead is added at the midway point of the braid after 40cm (16in). It is added to the bobbin in the position E(bottom). Use the instructions on the opposite page to create the effect shown in Fig 26.2.

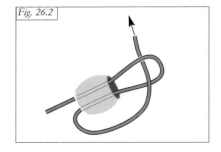

Fig. 26.2

Sample 26A

26. LOOPED ON-SINGLE

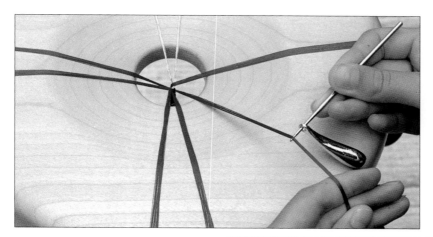

Take a crochet hook through the bead to pick up the warp threads on the bobbin in position E(bottom)

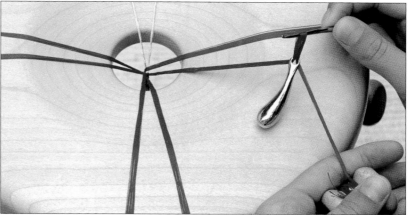

Pull the threads through the bead to create a loop.

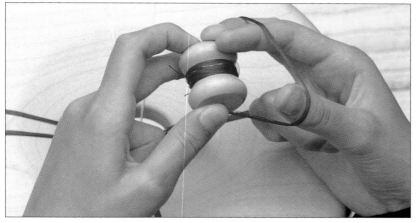

Take the bobbin through the loop.

Position the bead close to the braid before replacing the bobbin on the mirror.

SAMPLE 26B

BRAID DETAILS:

Braiding sequence: Spiral Braid One

Bobbin weight: 70gms (2½oz)

Weight bag: 275gms (10oz)

Finished length: 80cm (31in)

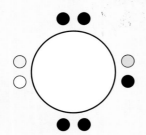

BEAD DETAILS:

1 black coloured metal pendant

  Bead size: 43x10mm(1⅔x¹³⁄₃₂in)

  Hole size: 3mm(⅛in)

WARP DETAILS:

● 20 strands of black Biron, 1.35m (53in) long

◐ 20 strands of yellow Biron, 1.35m (53in) long

○ 15 strands of silver metallised Biron, 1.35m (53in) long

○ 15 strands of gold metallised Biron, 1.35m (53in) long

WORKING: As Sample 26A

Sample 26B

26. LOOPED ON-SINGLE

SAMPLE 26C

BRAID DETAILS:

Braiding sequence: Spiral Braid One

Bobbin weight: 70gms (2½oz)

Weight bag: 275gms (10oz)

Finished length: 80cm (31in)

BEAD DETAILS:

1 silver coloured metal pendant
    Bead size: 43x10mm(1⅔x¹³⁄₃₂in)
    Hole size: 3mm(⅛in)

WARP DETAILS:

● 20 strands of red Biron, 1.35m (53in) long

● 20 strands of black Biron, 1.35m (53in) long

○ 15 strands of silver metallised Biron, 1.35m(53in) long

WORKING: As Sample 26A

Sample 26C

27 LOOPED ON-DOUBLE

These samples use the same idea of taking a loop of warp threads through the bead, although here two bobbins are used instead of one. This has the effect of balancing the bead between the two bobbins within the braid structure (see Fig 27.1).

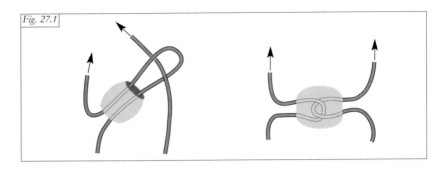

Fig. 27.1

SAMPLE 27A

BRAID DETAILS:

Braiding sequence: Ladder Braid

Bobbin weight: 100gms (3½oz)

Weight bag: 375gms (13oz)

Finished length: 75cm (29½in)

BEAD DETAILS:

65 pony gold glitter plastic

Bead size: 7x9mm(⁵⁄₃₂x¹¹⁄₃₂in)

Hole size: 4mm(⁵⁄₃₂in)

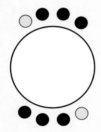

WARP DETAILS:

○ 40 strands of yellow Biron, 1.35m (53in) long

● 40 strands of black Biron, 1.35m (53in) long

WORKING

Repeat moves 1-4 of the ladder braid, three times. Now add a pony bead using the instructions on the opposite page.

Note that moves 5 and 6 of the ladder braid are not used for this sample.

It will not be possible to add beads at the end of the braid. This is because the knots holding the warp threads on to the bobbin leaders will prevent loops being made.

Sample 27A

27. LOOPED ON-DOUBLE

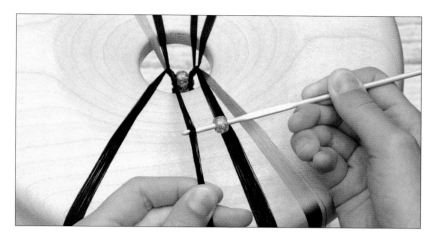

Pick up the warp threads from the bobbin in position S(inner left)

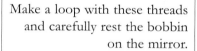

Make a loop with these threads and carefully rest the bobbin on the mirror.

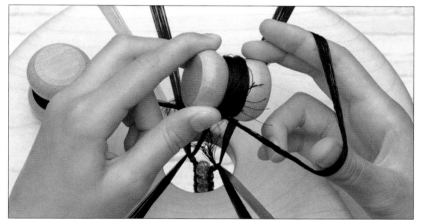

Take the bobbin from position N(inner right) through the loop before replacing it back in its original position.

Now lift the bobbin off the mirror and tension it, easing the bead into the point of braiding. Replace the bobbin back to its original position.

27. LOOPED ON-DOUBLE

SAMPLE 27B

BRAID DETAILS:

Braiding sequence: Ladder Braid

Bobbin weight: 100gms (3½oz)

Weight bag: 375gms (13oz)

Finished length: 75cm (29½in)

BEAD DETAILS:

30 pony gold coloured plastic
    Bead size: 7x9mm(⁹⁄₃₂x¹¹⁄₃₂in)
    Hole size: 4mm(⁵⁄₃₂in)

WARP DETAILS:

- ○ 40 strands of yellow Biron, 1.35m (53in) long
- ○ 40 strands of cream Biron, 1.35m (53in) long
- ● 40 strands of red Biron, 1.35m (53in) long

WORKING

This is worked in a similiar
manner to Sample 27A.

Work repeats of the following instructions:

Make three repeats of moves 1, 2, 3, 4.
Make moves 5,6.
Make three repeats of moves 1, 2, 3, 4.
Add a pony bead.

Sample 27B

27. LOOPED ON-DOUBLE

SAMPLE 27C

BRAID DETAILS:

Braiding sequence: Ladder Braid

Bobbin weight: 100gms (3½oz)

Weight bag: 375gms (13oz)

Finished length: 75cm (29½in)

WARP DETAILS:

● 40 strands of red Biron, 1.35m (53in) long

● 40 strands of black Biron, 1.35m (53in) long

BEAD DETAILS:

30 pony gold glitter plastic
  Bead size: 7x9mm(⁹⁄₃₂x¹¹⁄₃₂in) Hole size: 4mm(⁵⁄₃₂in)

15 'Sphere' - gold coloured plastic
  Bead size: 16mm(⅝in) Hole size: 4mm(⁵⁄₃₂in)

15 'Corrugated ring' - gold coloured plastic
  Bead size: 8x2mm(⁵⁄₁₆x⁵⁄₆₄in) Hole size: 4mm(⁵⁄₃₂in)

WORKING

The beads are added to the braid in the same manner as Sample 27A. One bead is added after every three repeats of moves 1-4 of the Ladder Braid. However, a different bead is added each time. First add a corrugated ring, then a pony bead followed by a sphere. Next add another pony bead before starting again with a corrugated ring.

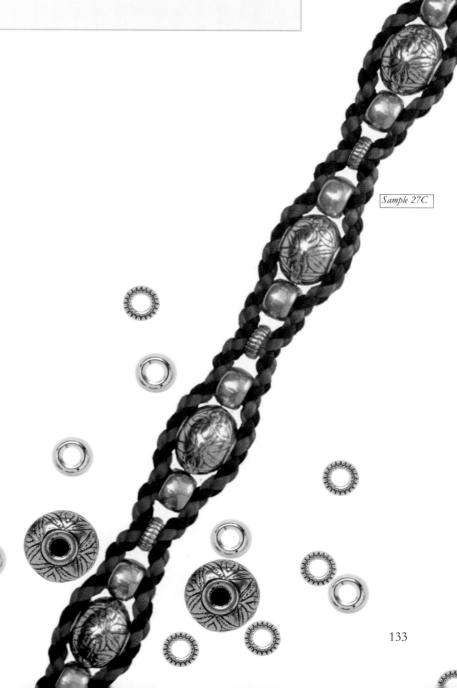

Sample 27C

133

28 LAID IN-STRINGS

A ready-made string of beads can be added to the braid simply by laying it across the point of braiding. When braiding is resumed the string gets trapped within the braid stitches. By altering where and when the beads cross the point of braiding, different effects are created.

SAMPLE 28A

BRAID DETAILS:

Braiding sequence: Flat Braid One

Bobbin weight: 100gms (3½oz)

Weight bag: 375gms (13oz)

Finished length: 80cm (31½in)

BEAD DETAILS:

1 string of gold plated beads
   Bead size: 2mm(⁵⁄₆₄in)
   String length: 120cm(47in)

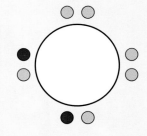

WARP DETAILS:

● 40 strands of navy Biron, 1.35m (53in) long
○ 40 strands of light blue Biron, 1.35m (53in) long

WORKING

Prepare the warp on to the bobbins. Prepare the string of beads separately. Then temporarily tie the end of the string on to the end of the warp threads; a half hitch should be sufficient. This will be removed when the braiding is complete so that the bead string can be securely sewn into the end of the braid.

Lay the string over the mirror so that it sits between the two bobbins in the South. The beads can be ignored whilst the braiding moves are made, just take the bobbins over and around them. Repeat the following:

Make two sequences of moves of Flat Braid One.
Then lift the beads over the point of braiding and lay them on the mirror between the two bobbins in the North (see Fig 28.1).
Work another two sequences of moves. Now lift the beads over the point of braiding back to their original position in the South (see Fig 28.2)

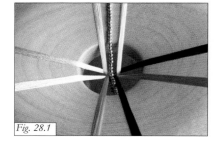
Fig. 28.1

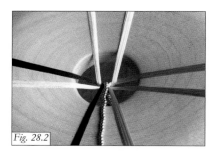
Fig. 28.2

Sample 28A

134

28. LAID IN-STRINGS

SAMPLE 28B

BRAID DETAILS:

Braiding sequence: Flat Braid One

Bobbin weight: 100gms (3½oz)

Weight bag: 375gms (13oz)

Finished length: 80cm (31½in)

BEAD DETAILS:

1 string of alternate turquoise frosted and
turquoise silver-lined rocaille

Bead size: 8/0

String length: 2m(79in)

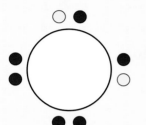

WARP DETAILS:

● 40 strands of blue Biron, 1.35m (53in) long

○ 30 strands of gold metallised Biron, 1.35m (53in) long

WORKING

Prepare the warp and tie on the string of beads. Once again the beads rest between the two bobbins in the South position. The sample is made by repeating the following instructions:

Work two sequences of moves. Then take the beads clockwise **under** all the bobbin threads until the beads arrive between the two bobbins in the North (see Fig 28.3). Now take the beads over the point of braiding back to their original position in the South. Work two more sequences of moves. Then take the beads anticlockwise, **under** the bobbin threads to the centre of North. Lift the beads over the point of braiding, back to their original position.

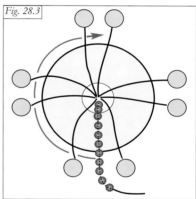

Fig. 28.3

Take the string of beads under four bobbins in a clockwise direction until you arrive in the North.

Sample 28B

28. LAID IN-STRINGS

SAMPLE 28C

BRAID DETAILS:

Braiding sequence: Flat Braid One

Bobbin weight: 100gms (3½oz)

Weight bag: 375gms (13oz)

Finished length: 80cm (31½in)

BEAD DETAILS:

2 strings of yellow silver-lined rocaille
   Bead size: 10/0 String length: 120cm(47in)

WARP DETAILS:

● 40 strands of navy Biron, 1.35m (53in) long

○ 30 strands of gold metallised Biron, 1.35m (53in) long

WORKING

Prepare the warp and both strings of beads. Place both strings on the mirror between the two bobbins in the South. Work the following:

Braid four sequences of moves. Take one string clockwise, under all the bobbin thread until the beads are between the two bobbins in the North. Take the other string, anticlockwise, under the bobbins until it reaches the first string (see Fig 28.4). Now take both strings over the point of braiding so that they are in their original places in the South.

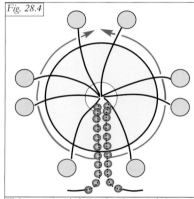

Fig. 28.4

Take one string clockwise, the other anti-clockwise under the bobbins to arrive in the North.

Sample 28C

29 LAID IN-TASSELS

These samples are worked using the same principle as used for the laid in strings, except here small units of beads are added independently.

To make the beaded tassels shown in Fig 29.1:-
Take a needle and thread through nineteen mauve rocaille beads then a black one. Go back through all nineteen mauve beads.

Now add a black bugle, nineteen mauve and a black rocaille. Go back through the most recently added nineteen mauve beads and the black bugle.

Add nineteen mauve and one black rocaille. Turn and go back through the mauve one and back through the bugle again.

Keep going in this manner until you have three strands of beads hanging out of each end of the bugle. Knot the ends of the thread and hide the ends inside the beads. Tip: the beads hang better if the tension is kept fairly loose.

Fig. 29.1

SAMPLE 29A

BRAID DETAILS:

Braiding sequence: Rectangular Braid
Bobbin weight: 100gms (3½oz)
Weight bag: 375gms (13oz)
Finished length: 70cm (27½in)

BEAD DETAILS:

18 black bugles
  Bead size: 4mm(⁵⁄₃₂in) long
2052 mauve iridescent rocaille
  Bead size: 10/0
108 black rocaille
  Bead size: 10/0

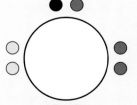

WARP DETAILS:

● 40 strands of purple Biron, 1.35m (53in) long
○ 40 strands of lilac Biron, 1.35m (53in) long
● 40 strands of black Biron, 1.35m (53in) long

29. LAID IN-TASSELS

WORKING

Prepare eighteen beaded tassels using the instructions given at the start of this section. *Make twelve sequences of moves. Now add a tassel so that it lies across the point of braiding between the two bobbins in the North and the two bobbins in the South (see Fig 29.2). Make two sequences of moves before adding another tassel in the same way. Braid another two sequences then add another tassel. Now repeat the instructions from *.

Fig. 29.2

Sample 29A

SAMPLE 29B

BEAD DETAILS:

33 black bugles
    Bead size: 4mm(⁵⁄₃₂in) long
3762 mauve iridescent rocaille
    Bead size: 10/0
198 black rocaille
    Bead size: 10/0

BRAID DETAILS:

Braiding sequence: Rectangular Braid
Bobbin weight: 100gms (3½oz)
Weight bag: 375gms (13oz)
Finished length: 70cm (27½in)

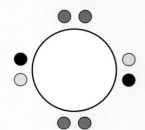

WARP DETAILS:

● 40 strands of purple Biron, 1.35m (53in) long
○ 40 strands of lilac Biron, 1.35m (53in) long
● 40 strands of black Biron, 1.35m (53in) long

29. LAID IN-TASSELS

WORKING

Prepare thirty-three beaded tassels.

Braid three sequences of moves then lay one tassel across the point of braiding so that it lies between the two bobbins in the North and two bobbins in the South. Continue braiding adding a tassel after every third sequence of moves.

Sample 29B

SAMPLE 29C

BRAID DETAILS:

Braiding sequence: Rectangular Braid

Bobbin weight: 100gms (3½oz)

Weight bag: 375gms (13oz)

Finished length: 70cm (27½in)

BEAD DETAILS:

33 black bugles   Bead size: 4mm(⁵⁄₃₂in) long

3762 mauve iridescent rocaille Bead size: 10/0

1188 black rocaille   Bead size: 10/0

198 gun metal drops   Bead size:10x5mm(¹³⁄₃₂x³⁄₁₆in)

WARP DETAILS:

● 40 strands of purple Biron, 1.35m (53in) long

○ 40 strands of lilac Biron, 1.35m (53in) long

● 40 strands of black Biron, 1.35m (53in) long

WORKING

Prepare thirty-three beaded tassels using the instructions given earlier except replace the single black rocaille with a series of three black rocaille, a drop and three more black rocaille.

Work the sample in the same manner as Sample 29B.

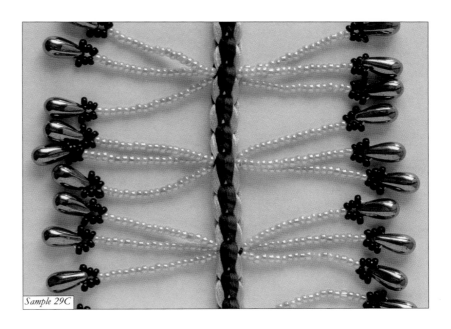

Sample 29C

30 SPLIT BRAID-DOUBLE

This technique works by making sections of braid that divide into two. The eight-bobbin braid becomes a pair of four-bobbin braids running parallel to each other. Beads are threaded on to these smaller braids before the two small braids re-unite to make an eight-bobbin braid. The effect is for the beads to get 'locked' into the braid. The disadvantage is that each bobbin must be removed in turn so that the warp threads can be sent through the bead. It is for this reason that the warp threads are not knotted on to the bobbin leaders until the last possible moment.

SAMPLE 30A

BRAID DETAILS:

Braiding sequence: Round Braid Two
Bobbin weight: 100gms (3½oz)
Weight bag: 375gms (13oz)
Finished length: 170cm (67in)

BEAD DETAILS:

100 'Corrugated rings' - gold coloured plastic
Bead size: 8x2mm(⁵⁄₁₆⁵⁄₆₄in)
Hole size: 4mm(⁵⁄₃₂in)

WARP DETAILS:

● 40 strands of blue Biron, 2.7m (9ft) long
● 40 strands of purple Biron, 2.7m (9ft) long
● 40 strands of black Biron, 2.7m (9ft) long

WORKING

Prepare the warp as normal but do not knot the threads on to the bobbin leaders. Simply wind the threads on to the bobbins and make the slip knot to prevent them unravelling.

Work fourteen sequences of the Round Braid Two. The braid is then split along the line indicated in Fig. 30.1. Rearrange the bobbins by sliding them round the mirror until they are in the positions shown in Fig 30.2.

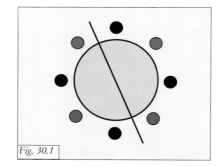
Fig. 30.1

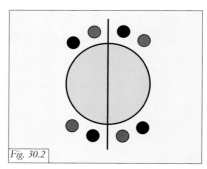
Fig. 30.2

Sample 30A

140

30. SPLIT BRAID-DOUBLE

Now work fourteen sequences of moves 1, 2, 3 and 4 of the Ladder Braid. This creates two fine, four-bobbin braids (see Fig 30.3).

To add the beads, take the bobbin in the North (furthest left). Remove the threads from the bobbin and take them through a series of five ring beads (see Fig 30.4). Use a crochet hook or a piece of spare thread to help. This is similar to the method shown on page 126 except the threads do not just form a loop but are pulled right through the bead.

When the threads are through the beads, rejoin the bobbin and replace it across the mirror making sure it returns to the same place it came from (see Fig 30.5).

Now take the bobbin in the North (inner left) position and take it through the same set of beads in the same way (see Fig 30.6). Repeat this with the bobbin in position South (inner left).

Finally remove the bobbin in the South (furthest left). Push the beads down on to the small braid and these last threads can be easily pulled through the beads and returned on to the bobbin (see Fig 30.7).

Fig. 30.3

Five ring beads can now be added to the fine braid on the right-hand side in the same way. When the beads are on each fine braid and all the threads are back on the bobbins, slide the bobbins back to their original positions.

The two fine braids are rejoined when you start to repeat the instructions. Some of the threads may require extra tensioning at this point. Note that as the braid nears completion, the threads will need to be knotted on to the bobbin leaders to prevent them falling off.

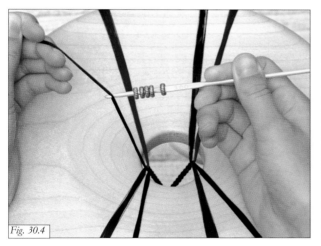

Fig. 30.4

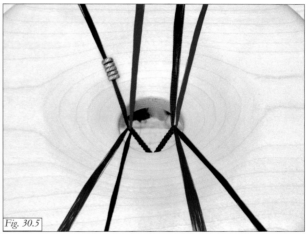

Fig. 30.5

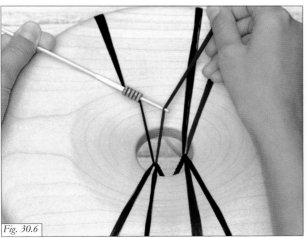

Fig. 30.6

Fig. 30.7

30. SPLIT BRAID-DOUBLE

SAMPLE 30B

BRAID DETAILS:

Braiding sequence: Round Braid Two

Bobbin weight: 100gms (3½oz)

Weight bag: 375gms (13oz)

Finished length: 170cm (67in)

BEAD DETAILS:

20 'Amber' - round acrylic
Bead size: 18mm(^{23}⁄₃₂in) Hole size: 4mm(^{5}⁄₃₂in)

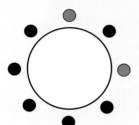

WARP DETAILS:

- 40 strands of rust Biron, 2.7m (9ft) long
- 40 strands of black Biron, 2.7m (9ft) long

WORKING

Work fourteen sequences of Round Braid Two. Split the braid by rearranging the bobbins as shown in Fig 30.8 and working fourteen sequences of moves 1, 2, 3 and 4 of the Ladder Braid. Add a single bead over each of the fine braids (by taking the thread from each bobbin through the bead in turn.)

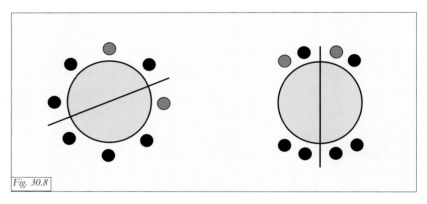

Fig. 30.8

Sample 30B

30. SPLIT BRAID-DOUBLE

SAMPLE 30C

BRAID DETAILS:

Braiding sequence: Round Braid Two

Bobbin weight: 70gms (2½oz)

Weight bag: 275gms (10oz)

Finished length: 85cm (33in)

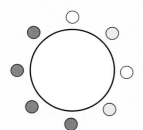

BEAD DETAILS:

7 different semi-precious stone arrowheads
  Bead size: 30x15mm(1³⁄₁₆x¹⁹⁄₃₂in)
  Hole size: 2mm(⁵⁄₆₄in)

WARP DETAILS:

- 10 strands of rust Biron, 1.35m (53in) long
- 10 strands of yellow Biron, 1.35m (53in) long
- 10 strands of cream Biron, 1.35m (53in) long

WORKING

Work 32cm of Round Braid Two.

* Split the braid by rearranging the bobbins in the same manner as Sample 30A (see Fig 30.1 & 2). Work seven sequences of moves 1, 2, 3 and 4 of the Ladder Braid. Now add an arrowhead bead on to the right-hand fine braid (the left-hand braid remains untouched).

Now work six sequences of the Round Braid Two and repeat from *. Note that the arrowhead beads have two distinct sides so make sure they are all added the same way round.

When all seven beads have been added, finish with a final section of Round Braid Two.

Sample 30C

31 SPLIT BRAID-SINGLE

These are similar to the double version except here only one four-bobbin braid is made whilst the other four bobbins remain static. Beads are added to the small braid before braiding continues with all eight bobbins. The result is a fine, four-bobbin braid forming a loop extension on which the beads sit. Once again, the bobbins have to be removed in order to get the thread through the beads. Because of this the threads are not knotted on to the bobbin leaders until the last possible moment.

SAMPLE 31A

BRAID DETAILS:

Braiding sequence: Round Braid One

Bobbin weight: 70gms (2½oz)

Weight bag: 275gms (10oz)

Finished length: 65cm (26in)

BEAD DETAILS:

4 'Flat fish' - coloured glass
    Bead size: 25x16mm(1$_x$⅝in)
    Hole size: 3mm(⅛in)
1 'Long fish' - coloured glass
    Beads size: 45x16mm(1^{25}₃₂x⅝in)
    Hole size: 3mm(⅛in)

WARP DETAILS:

● 20 strands of green silk, 1.35m (53in) long
○ 20 strands of white silk, 1.35m (53in) long

WORKING

Make 25cm(10in) of Round Braid One.

* The braid is split, working sixteen sequences of moves 1 and 2 of the Ladder Braid with the bobbins in positions North and South. This raises the point of braiding. Help it to settle by manually pulling the braid down from below the mirror. Add the fish bead on to this fine braid by taking the threads from each bobbin through the bead in turn (as seen in Sample 30A)

Now work twenty sequences of Round Braid One. It will take a couple of sequences for the point of braiding to settle and extra tensioning will be required to take up the slack at this point where the fine braid rejoins the main braid. Repeat from * until all the beads are on the braid. Add the beads in the following order: flat, flat, long, flat and flat. Finish with a section of Round Braid One.

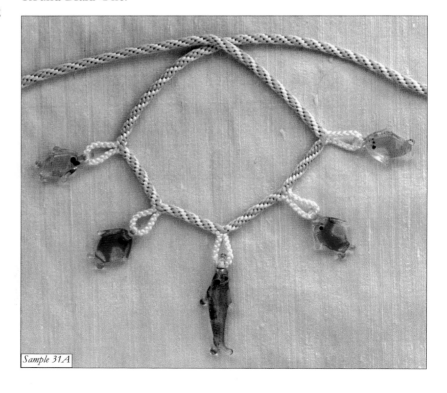

Sample 31A

31. SPLIT BRAID-SINGLE

SAMPLE 31B

BRAID DETAILS:

Braiding sequence: Round Braid One

Bobbin weight: 70gms (2½oz)

Weight bag: 275gms (10oz)

Finished length: 60cm (23½in)

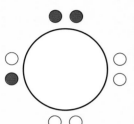

BEAD DETAILS:

3 'Fish' - carved soapstone

   Bead size: 43x15mm(1$^{23}/_{32}$x$^{19}/_{32}$in)

   Hole size: 3mm(⅛in)

WARP DETAILS:

● 10 strands of burgundy Biron, 1.35m (53in) long

○ 10 strands of white Biron, 1.35m (53in) long

WORKING

Make 25cm(10in) of Round Braid One.

* Split the braid by working twenty sequences of moves 3 and 4 of the Ladder Braid with the bobbins in positions East and South. This is easier to do if the East bobbins are slid around the mirror until they are in the North (don't forget to move them back when the four-bobbin braid is complete). Add a single fish bead on to this fine braid and rejoin to the main braid by working eight sequences of Round Braid One. Repeat from * two more times before ending with a section of Round Braid One.

Sample 31B

SAMPLE 31C

BRAID DETAILS:

Braiding sequence: Round Braid One

Bobbin weight: 70gms (2½oz)

Weight bag: 275gms (10oz)

Finished length: 60cm (23½in)

BEAD DETAILS:

10 silver-plated acrylic ring
  Bead size:10x2mm(¹³⁄₃₂x⁵⁄₆₄in) Hole size: 4mm(⁵⁄₃₂in)
10 silver-plated acrylic ring
  Bead size: 8x2mm(⁵⁄₁₆x⁵⁄₆₄in) Hole size: 3mm(⅛in)
5 silver-plated metal petroglyph charms
  Beads size: 30x15mm(1³⁄₁₆x¹⁹⁄₃₂in)

WARP DETAILS:

● 40 strands of grey silk, 1.35m (53in) long

● 10 strands of pink silk, 1.35m (53in) long

WORKING

Work 20cm(8in) of Round Braid One.

* Split the braid, working thirty sequences of moves 3 and 4 of the Ladder Braid with the bobbins in positions North and East (you may wish to re-arrange these bobbins so that they lie North and South).

Add the beads on to the fine braid in the correct order: large ring, small ring, charm, small ring and large ring. Work twenty sequences of Round Braid One and repeat from *

Finish with a section of Round Braid One. Note that the charms are one sided and need to be added the same way round.

Sample 31C

146

32 SPLIT BRAID-CORE

The braid is worked over a beading thread so that the beading thread forms an inner core running through the interior of the braid (see Fig 32.1).

Once again the braid is split by working a pair of four-bobbin braids but this time the beads are added on to the inner core beading thread so that they sit between the two fine braids. When the eight-bobbin braid is resumed, the beading thread returns to be hidden inside it.

An overhead support point for the internal thread will help

Fig 32.1

Braiding around an inner core of beading thread.

enormously. It is possible to work with the inner core resting over your shoulder but ideally it should be directly over the point of braiding and counterbalanced so that it drops smoothly down with the braid. An angle poise lamp can provide a point over which to hang the inner core.

Unlike the previous split braids the warp threads do not have to be threaded through the beads. Due to this, the warp threads can be knotted on to the bobbin leaders at the start.

SAMPLE 32A

BRAID DETAILS:

Braiding sequence: Round Braid Two

Bobbin weight: 70gms (2½oz)

Weight bag: 275gms (10oz)

Finished length: 85cm (33½in)

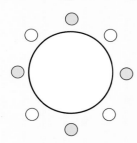

BEAD DETAILS:

70 'Sunbursts' - gold coloured, star-shaped plastic
Bead size: 10x4mm($^{13}⁄_{32}$x$^5⁄_{32}$in)

WARP DETAILS:

○ 10 strands of yellow Biron, 1.35m (53in) long
○ 10 strands of cream Biron, 1.35m (53in) long

WORKING

Prepare a warp as shown. Temporarily tie the beading thread securely on to the end of the warp threads. This can be permanently sewn into the braid when work is complete and the ends are being whipped.

Lift the beading thread above the point of braiding so that it will become the inner core of

the braid. Now make fifteen sequences of Round Braid Two. Work around the inner core making sure that it is running straight and tight up the centre of the braid.

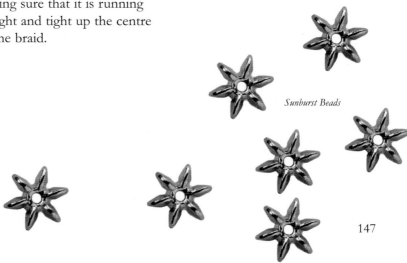

Sunburst Beads

32. SPLIT BRAID-CORE

To split the braid, re-arrange the bobbins as shown in Fig 32.2. Lay the beading thread on to the surface of the mirror so that it rests between the two inner South bobbins.

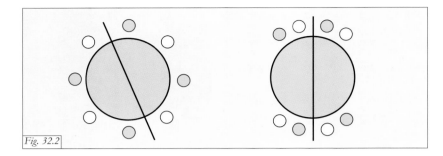

Fig. 32.2

Fig. 32.3

Make nine sequences of the moves 1, 2, 3 and 4 of the Ladder Braid. Add a cluster of five beads on to the beading thread. You are now ready to start repeating the instructions, with the beading thread returning to its original position above the point of braiding (see Fig 32.3). It is worth pausing after the first sequence of Round Braid Two to make sure that the beads are sitting evenly between the pair of fine braids. Extra tensioning may be required to take up any slack at this rejoining point.

Sample 32A

SAMPLE 32B

BRAID DETAILS:

Braiding sequence: Round Braid Two

Bobbin weight: 70gms (2½oz)

Weight bag: 275gms (10oz)

Finished length: 80cm (31½in)

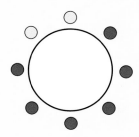

BEAD DETAILS:

30 'Hearts' - black design on white acrylic
Bead size: 15x13x8mm($^{19}/_{32}$x$^{33}/_{64}$x$^{5}/_{16}$in)

WARP DETAILS:

○ 10 strands of pink silk, 1.35m (53in) long

● 10 strands of burgundy silk, 1.35m (53in) long

WORKING

This sample is worked in the same manner as Sample 32A except here, six repeats of Round Braid Two are made before splitting the braid along the division line shown in Fig 32.4. Eight repeats of moves 1-4 of the Ladder braid are made before starting the process again.

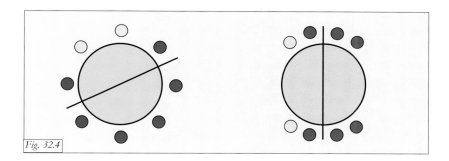

Fig. 32.4

Sample 32B

32. SPLIT BRAID-CORE

SAMPLE 32C

BRAID DETAILS:

Braiding sequence: Round Braid Two

Bobbin weight: 70gms (2½oz)

Weight bag: 275gms (10oz)

Finished length: 80cm (31½in)

BEAD DETAILS:

25 'Triangles' - Rose Quartz, semi-precious stone
Bead size: 18x4mm($^{23}/_{32}$x$^{5}/_{32}$in)

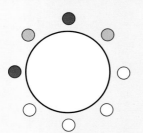

WARP DETAILS:

○ 16 strands of pale pink silk, 1.35m (53in) long

◐ 16 strands of pink silk, 1.35m (53in) long

● 12 strands of variegated metallic Biron, 1.35m (53in) long

WORKING

This sample is worked in the same manner as Sample 32A except here, six repeats of Round Braid Two are made before splitting the braid along the division line shown in Fig 32.5. Eight repeats of moves 1-4 of the Ladder braid are made before starting the process again.

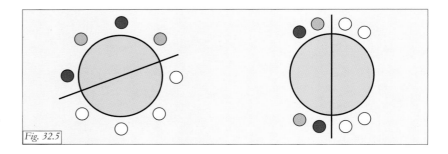

Fig. 32.5

Sample 32C

33 BEADED CORE

This is not a true 'beading during braiding' as it is a combination of 'before and after'. A round braid is completed in advance. It is then re-used as an inner core for a second braid, which has a beaded warp. The inner core braid can lie on the mirror so an overhead support point is not required. The second braid has beads added on to its warp threads before work starts.

The inner core braid for each sample is made in advance using the adjoining specifications.

BRAID DETAILS:

Braiding sequence: Round Braid One

Bobbin weight: 100gms (3½oz)

Weight bag: 400gms (14oz)

WARP DETAILS:

● 40 strands of black Biron

● 40 strands of green Biron

SAMPLE 33A

BEAD DETAILS:

2 strings of black rocaille
    Bead size: 10/0 String length: 135cm(53in)

BRAID DETAILS:

Braiding sequence: Ladder Braid

Bobbin weight: 100gms (3½oz)

Weight bag: 400gms (14oz)

Finished length: 1m (39in)

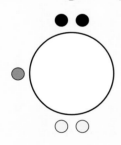

WARP DETAILS:

◐ 1 pre-made braid 115cm (45in) long

○ 30 strands of gold metallised Biron, 1.35m (53in) long

● String of black beads 135cm(53in)

WORKING

Tie the warp and pre-made braid together. Attach bobbins to the warp threads and to the pre-made braid. Position the pre-made braid in the West.

 * Make moves 1 and 2 of the Ladder Braid with the bead strings and gold thread. Now move the pre-made braid from the West to the East (see Fig 33.1 and Fig 33.2). Make moves 1 and 2 of the Ladder Braid before returning the braid back to its original position. Repeat from *

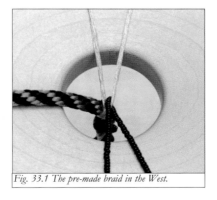

Fig. 33.1 The pre-made braid in the West.

Fig. 33.2 The pre-made braid in the East.

33. BEADED CORE

Sample 33A

SAMPLE 33B

BRAID DETAILS:

Braiding sequence: Ladder Braid

Bobbin weight: 100gms (3½oz)

Weight bag: 400gms (14oz)

Finished length: 1m (39in)

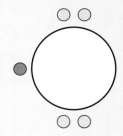

BEAD DETAILS:

800 green iridescent, silver-lined rocaille
　　Bead size: 8/0

WARP DETAILS:

● 1 pre-made braid 115cm (45in) long

○ 16 strands of green Biron, 1.35m (53in) long -
　　threaded with 200 x beads

33. BEADED CORE

WORKING

Make moves 1,2,1,2 of the Ladder Braid. Add seven beads from every beaded bobbin, then move the pre-made braid from West to East.

Make moves 1,2,1,2 of the Ladder Braid. Add seven beads from every beaded bobbin, then move the pre-made braid from East to West.

Repeat the whole process until the end of the braid.

Sample 33B

SAMPLE 33C

BRAID DETAILS:

Braiding sequence: Ladder Braid

Bobbin weight: 100gms (3½oz)

Weight bag: 400gms (14oz)

Finished length: 1m (39in)

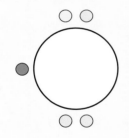

BEAD DETAILS:

1 string of gold-plated metal
   Bead size: 2mm(⁵⁄₆₄in) String length: 135cm(53in)
3 strings of green, iridescent, silver-lined rocaille
   Bead size: 8/0 String length: 135cm(53in)

WARP DETAILS:

● 1 pre-made braid 115cm (45in) long
○ String of gold beads 135cm(53in) long
○ String of green beads 135cm (53in) long

WORKING

Make moves 1 and 2 of the Ladder Braid . Take the pre-made braid from West to East.
Make moves 1 and 2 of the Ladder braid, then take the pre-made braid from East to West.

Sample 33C

A carved agate pendant looped
on to a beaded braid.

Amber beads looped on to the silk
braid during the braiding process.

Strings of rocaille beads have been laid into the braid during its production.

Bead tassels, made from painted pasta,
have been laid into the silk braid necklace.

The lampwork 'Eye' bead is enclosed
within the split (and knotted) silk braid.

A single split braid incorporating a lampwork bead.

GALLERY 32

Necklaces made from
braids splitting around
the grooved glass beads.

Beaded warps braided over inner core braids.

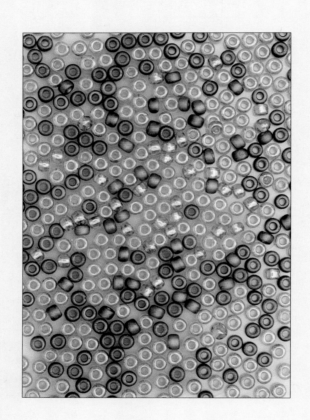

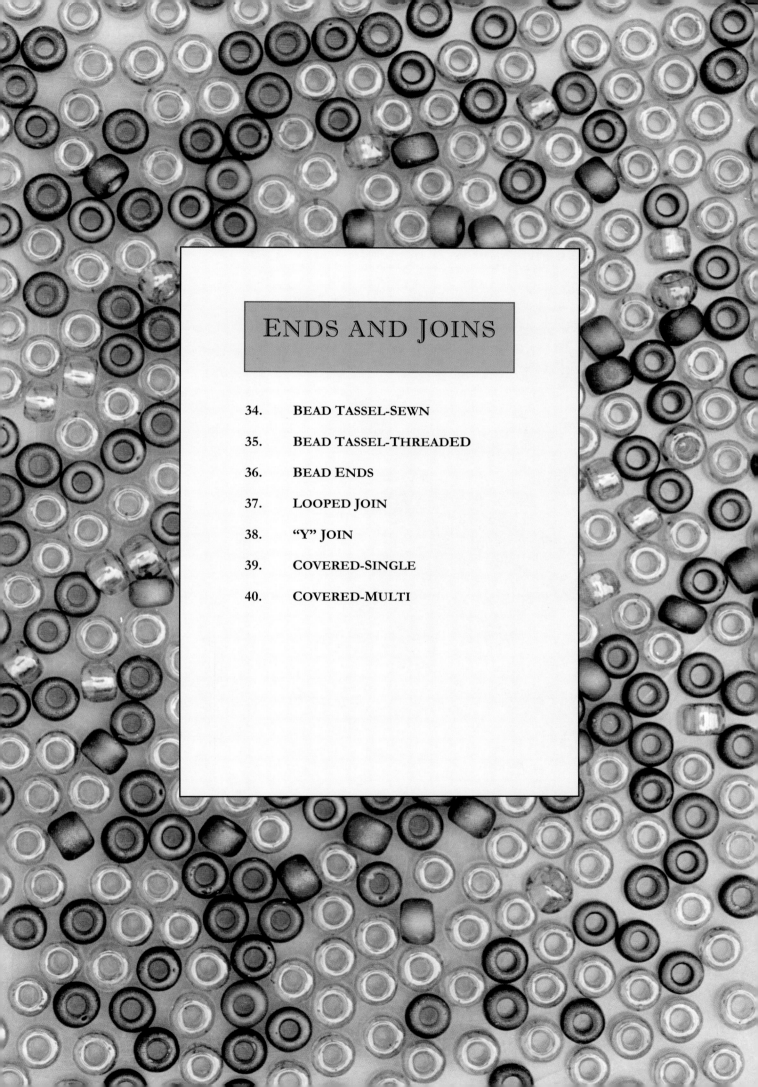

ENDS AND JOINS

34 BEAD TASSEL-SEWN

This is a very adaptable technique as beaded skirts can be sewn over any braid tassel. Any bead type can be added to the tassel to complement and finish the project. The beads can be sewn on using any thread but these samples use a double thickness of Biron, with the colour chosen to match the whipping.

Sample 34A

SAMPLE 34A

BRAID DETAILS:

Braiding sequence: Spiral Braid Two
Bobbin weight: 100gms (3½oz)
Weight bag: 375gms (13oz)

BEAD DETAILS:

270 yellow colour-lined rocaille
    Bead size: 8/0
9 gold-plated metal
    Bead size: 3mm(⅛in)

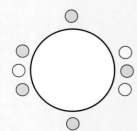

WARP DETAILS:

- 40 strands of yellow Biron
- 30 strands of gold metallised Biron

34. BEAD TASSEL-SEWN

WORKING

Make a braid using the details shown. Whip the end in the usual manner, then steam and trim the tassel.

Thread a beading needle with two strands of yellow Biron and secure it into the braid just above the whipping. Take the needle and thread through thirty yellow beads and finally through one gold bead. Now go back through all the yellow beads. Take the needle and thread through the braid to secure the newly created strand of beads(see Fig 34.1).

Make another strand of beads next to the first and continue around the braid until a full circle of strands hang down over the tassel of warp threads.

Fig. 34.1

SAMPLE 34B

BRAID DETAILS:

Braiding sequence: Spiral Braid Two
Bobbin weight: 100gms (3½oz)
Weight bag: 375gms (13oz)

BEAD DETAILS:

108 blue bugles
    Bead size: 4mm(⁵⁄₃₂in)long
9 gold-plated metal
    Bead size: 2mm(³⁄₃₂in)

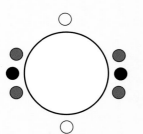

WARP DETAILS:

- 🔵 40 strands of blue Biron
- ⚫ 40 strands of black Biron
- ⚪ 30 strands of gold metallised Biron

WORKING

Work in the same manner as Sample 34A except replace the thirty yellow beads with twelve bugle beads.

Sample 34B

34. BEAD TASSEL-SEWN

SAMPLE 34C

BEAD DETAILS:

200 yellow colour-lined rocaille
  Bead size: 8/0
180 gold-plated metal
  Bead size: 2mm(⁵⁄₆₄in)
10 'Amber' glass drops
  Bead size: 15x5mm(¹⁹⁄₃₂³⁄₁₆in)

BRAID DETAILS:

Braiding sequence: Spiral Braid Two
Bobbin weight: 100gms (3½oz)
Weight bag: 375gms (13oz)

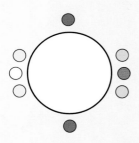

WARP DETAILS:

⬤ 30 strands of gold metallised Biron
⬤ 40 strands of deep yellow Biron
◯ 40 strands of yellow Biron
◯ 40 strands of pale yellow Biron
◯ 40 strands of cream Biron

WORKING

This tassel is worked with alternate yellow and gold beads. Take the thread through thirty-one beads (start and end with a yellow bead). Now add a drop bead. Add seven more alternate beads (again, start and end with a yellow one). Now go back into the twenty-fourth bead (a gold one) and back up all the previous beads. Finally go back into the braid. Repeat until ten of these strands have been made around the braid.

Sample 34C

35 BEAD TASSEL-THREADED

Here the beads are threaded directly on to the warp threads. This can be done after the braiding is complete, but it is easier to do it whilst preparing the warp. Beads are added to the warp threads in the same manner as shown on page 72. It is therefore a sympathetic finish to use on braids of this type. The samples here show a beaded tassel on the end of the braid but it is also possible to have another one at the beginning.

Sample 35A

SAMPLE 35A

BRAID DETAILS:

Braiding sequence: Flat Braid Two

Bobbin weight: 70gms (2½oz)

Weight bag: 275gms (10oz)

BEAD DETAILS:

240 purple, frosted iridescent rocaille
Bead size: 10/0

WARP DETAILS:

- 16 strands of purple silk - threaded with 30 x purple beads
- 16 strands of turquoise silk - threaded with 30 x purple beads
- 16 strands of light blue silk - threaded with 30 x purple beads
- 16 strands of lilac silk - threaded with 30 x purple beads

WORKING

Whilst preparing the warp, add thirty beads on to the threads for each bobbin. Make the braid keeping these beads on the end of the warp threads closest to the bobbin.

At the end of the braiding process, temporarily tie the braid to stop it unravelling. Remove the bobbins and weight bag, making sure that the beads stay on the warp threads.

35. BEAD TASSEL-THREADED

Whip the end of the braid (see Fig 35.1). Push the beads up the warp threads towards the whipping and make an overhand knot in the threads to keep the beads in place (see Fig 35.2). The friction of the natural fibres will be sufficient to hold the knot in place, although dampening the threads will also help to make the knot firm. If synthetic threads are to be used, a small amount of glue over the knot will provide the necessary security.

Fig. 35.1

Fig. 35.2

SAMPLE 35B

BEAD DETAILS:

120 purple, frosted iridescent rocaille
    Bead size: 10/0
120 turquoise, frosted iridescent rocaille
    Bead size: 10/0

BRAID DETAILS:

Braiding sequence: Flat Braid Two
Bobbin weight: 70gms (2½oz)
Weight bag: 275gms (10oz)

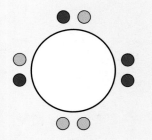

WARP DETAILS:

● 16 strands of purple silk -
    threaded with 30 x purple beads
○ 16 strands of light blue silk -
    threaded with 30 x turquoise beads

WORKING

This is worked in exactly the same way as Sample 35A, although this sample uses different coloured beads on the different coloured warp threads.

35. BEAD TASSEL-THREADED

SAMPLE 35C

BRAID DETAILS:

Braiding sequence: Flat Braid Two

Bobbin weight: 70gms (2½oz)

Weight bag: 275gms (10oz)

BEAD DETAILS:

120 'T' - Turquoise, silver-lined rocaille
   Bead size: 8/0
120 'P' - Purple Delica
   Bead size: 11/0

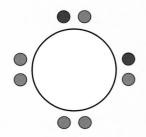

WARP DETAILS:

● 16 strands of purple silk
   threaded with 30 x alternate 'P' & 'T' beads
● 16 strands of turquoise silk
   threaded with 30 'P' & 'T' beads

WORKING

This is worked in exactly the same way as Sample 35A, but uses alternate coloured beads on the warp threads.

Sample 35C

Sample 35B

36 BEAD ENDS

This technique uses the same principle as Bell caps (see page 48) except beads are used instead of bell caps. The large beads have a hole size large enough to accommodate the braid in one end. The small black bead is used to fill the other end to give a neat, flush finish.

SAMPLE 36A

BEAD DETAILS:

1 'Pony' - gold coloured plastic
    Bead size: 7x9mm(⁹⁄₃₂¹¹⁄₃₂in) Hole size: 4mm(⁵⁄₃₂in)
1 black round glass
    Bead size: 4mm(⁵⁄₃₂in)

BRAID DETAILS:

Braiding sequence: Round Braid One
Bobbin weight: 70gms (2½oz)
Weight bag: 275gms (10oz)

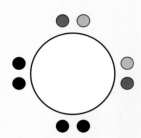

WARP DETAILS:

- ● 20 strands of black Biron
- ● 20 strands of red Biron
- ● 20 strands of orange Biron

WORKING

Use a braid as described. Whip the end of the braid and trim away any tassel threads. Position the black bead in the end of the pony bead and rest the two beads on a piece of modelling clay or similar. This will hold everything in place until the glue dries. Next, partially fill the pony bead with a suitable adhesive and push the braid into the open end of the bead. Leave to dry.

The Pony bead is filled with glue and held in position whilst the braid is fitted into the open end of the bead.

Sample 36A

36. BEAD ENDS

SAMPLE 36B

BRAID DETAILS:

Braiding sequence: Round Braid One

Bobbin weight: 70gms (2½oz)

Weight bag: 275gms (10oz)

BEAD DETAILS:

1 'Melon' - gold coloured plastic
    Bead size: 10mm(¹³⁄₃₂in) Hole size: 4mm(⁵⁄₃₂in)
1 black round glass
    Bead size: 4mm(⁵⁄₆₄in)

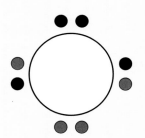

WARP DETAILS:

● 20 strands of black Biron
● 20 strands of red Biron

WORKING: As Sample 36A

Sample 36B

SAMPLE 36C

BRAID DETAILS:

Braiding sequence: Round Braid One

Bobbin weight: 70gms (2½oz)

Weight bag: 275gms (10oz)

BEAD DETAILS:

1 'Sphere' - gold coloured plastic
    Bead size: 16mm(⁵⁄₈in) Hole size: 4mm(⁵⁄₃₂in)
1 black round glass.
    Bead size: 4mm(⁵⁄₆₄in)

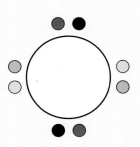

WARP DETAILS:

● 20 strands of black Biron
● 20 strands of red Biron
● 20 strands of orange Biron
○ 20 strands of yellow Biron

WORKING: As Sample 36A

Sample 36C

37 LOOPED JOIN

A 'toggle' effect can be created with a bead and a loop of braid. This can then be used to join the two ends of a braid together. Three variations on this theme are shown in the following samples. All three of them use beads that are threaded on to the braid. The braid is then turned back on itself to form the loop.

SAMPLE 37A

BRAID DETAILS:

Braiding sequence: Flat Braid One
Bobbin weight: 70gms (2½oz)
Weight bag: 275gms (10oz)

BEAD DETAILS:

1 'Ring' silver-plated plastic
Bead size: 14x5mm(⁹⁄₁₆x³⁄₁₆in)
Hole size: 4mm(⁵⁄₃₂in)

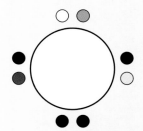

WARP DETAILS:

- ● 16 strands of black silk
- ● 16 strands of burgundy silk
- ● 16 strands of pink silk
- ○ 16 strands of pale pink silk
- ○ 16 strands of white silk

WORKING

Thread the bead on to one end of the braid. Fold the braid back on itself so that it forms a loop with the bead enclosed in it. Sew the braid end down and neatly whip over the join.

A plain loop of braid is made on the other end of the braid. Make sure it is just large enough for the bead to be slipped through it.

Sample 37A

172

37. LOOPED JOIN

SAMPLE 37B

BRAID DETAILS:

Braiding sequence: Flat Braid One

Bobbin weight: 70gms (2½oz)

Weight bag: 275gms (10oz)

BEAD DETAILS:

2 'Lozenge' silver-coated acrylic
  Bead size: 25x10mm($1_x^{13}\!/\!_{32}$in)
  Hole size: 4mm($^5\!/\!_{32}$in)

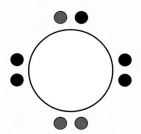

WARP DETAILS:

● 16 strands of black silk

● 16 strands of burgundy silk

WORKING

The working method is the same as Sample 37A except a bead is added on to each loop.

Sample 37B

37. LOOPED JOIN

SAMPLE 37C

BRAID DETAILS:

Braiding sequence: Flat Braid One

Bobbin weight: 70gms (2½oz)

Weight bag: 275gms (10oz)

BEAD DETAILS:

2 'Pony' gold coloured plastic
  Bead size: 7x9mm(⁹⁄₃₂¹¹⁄₃₂in)
  Hole size: 4mm(⁵⁄₃₂in)

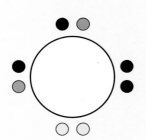

WARP DETAILS:

● 16 strands of black silk

● 16 strands of pink silk

○ 16 strands of pale pink silk

WORKING

This variation produces a join that can be adjusted to alter the length. Both beads are added on to the end of the braid. The first bead is pushed along the braid out of the way. The other bead is added to the braid and enclosed in the loop in the same way as Sample 37A.

When the loop is secure, bring the first bead back over this sewing. The other end of

Sample 37C

the braid is left in a straightforward tassel that can be taken through the loop. The first bead can be pushed towards the end tightening the loop and securing the join.

38 "Y" JOIN

Here both of the braids are brought together by whipping over them both and creating one tassel out of their warp threads. The beads can then be fixed over this join to make a decorative feature.

The beads can be prevented from slipping off the end but left free to travel up the braids. The beads can then be used to adjust the length of the piece.

SAMPLE 38A

BRAID DETAILS:

Braiding sequence: Spiral Braid One

Bobbin weight: 70gms (2½oz)

Weight bag: 275gms (10oz)

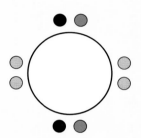

WARP DETAILS:

- 8 strands of green silk
- 8 strands of black silk
- 16 strands of grey silk

BEAD DETAILS:

1 'Sphere' - black design on white acrylic
    Bead size: 16mm(⅝in) Hole size: 4mm(⁵⁄₃₂in)

WORKING

Thread both ends of the braid through the bead. Bring the two ends together and whip over them both (See Fig 38.1). Steam and trim the resulting tassel. The bead can now be slid down to cover the join. Friction will hold the bead in place but a permanent fixing can be achieved by placing a small amount of glue on the whipping prior to sliding the bead over it.

Fig. 38.1

Sample 38A

SAMPLE 38B

BRAID DETAILS:

Braiding sequence: Spiral Braid One

Bobbin weight: 70gms (2½oz)

Weight bag: 275gms (10oz)

BEAD DETAILS:

1 'Sphere' - black design on white acrylic
    Bead size: 16mm(⅝in) Hole size: 4mm(⁵⁄₃₂in)
10 black rocaille
    Bead size: 10/0

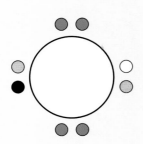

WARP DETAILS:

- 8 strands of green silk
- 16 strands of black silk
- 16 strands of grey silk
- 16 strands of white silk

WORKING

Add the large bead over the two braid ends and whip to join the ends together. Secure the end of the whipping thread but do not remove it. Instead, take it through ten small black beads. Wrap them around the whipping and then take the needle and thread through the first few beads again (going in the same direction). Tighten the thread so that the beads form a small circle around the braid. This can be further secured by taking the needle and thread back into the braid and sewing a couple of securing stitches. This small ring of beads will prevent the larger bead from dropping off the tassel end.

Sample 38B

SAMPLE 38C

BRAID DETAILS:

Braiding sequence: Spiral Braid One

Bobbin weight: 70gms (2½oz)

Weight bag: 275gms (10oz)

BEAD DETAILS:

5 'Rings' - silver-coated acrylic
    Bead size: 16x4mm(⅝x⁵⁄₃₂in)
    Hole size: 8mm(⁵⁄₁₆in)
1 Black glass bead
    Bead size: 6mm (¼in)

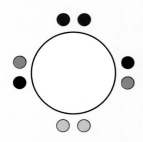

WARP DETAILS:

- ● 40 strands of navy silk
- ● 20 strands of navy silk
- ● 40 strands of green silk
- ○ 20 strands of green silk

WORKING

The five ring beads are added over the two braid ends. The ends are whipped and the large black bead is sewn into position at the centre of the tassel below the whipping. Do this by taking the needle and thread below the whipping, through the bead, and

The bead hidden at the centre of the tassel.

Sample 38C

back up into the braid above the whipping. This forms a hidden stopper for the five ring beads and helps to fluff up the tassel.

39 COVERED-SINGLE

The two ends of a braid can be joined together by sewing or gluing them. This join can then be hidden under a single bead. These can be added on to the braid before the join is made or they can be attached afterwards as Sample 39C shows.

This style of join can look particularly effective if the braid has been threaded with similar beads. This disguises the join, making the braid appear as a continuous piece.

SAMPLE 39A

BRAID DETAILS:

Braiding sequence: Square Braid
Bobbin weight: 70gms (2½oz)
Weight bag: 275gms (10oz)

BEAD DETAILS:

1 'Lozenge' - gold-coated acrylic
    Bead size: 25x10mm(1x^{13}⁄₃₂in)
    Hole size: 4mm(⁵⁄₃₂in)

WARP DETAILS:

● 20 strands of brown silk
◑ 20 strands of tan silk
○ 20 strands of cream silk

WORKING

Whip both ends of the braid and trim away the tassel ends. Place some glue into the bead and push one end of the braid into the bead hole (see Fig 39.1). Now fit the other end of the braid into the opposite end of the bead and wait for the glue to dry.

Fig. 39.1

Sample 39A - the join is hidden under one of the beads.

39. COVERED- SINGLE

SAMPLE 39B

BRAID DETAILS:

Braiding sequence: Square Braid

Bobbin weight: 70gms (2½oz)

Weight bag: 275gms (10oz)

BEAD DETAILS:

1 'Lozenge' - gold-coated acrylic
  Bead size: 25x10mm(1x^{13}⁄₃₂in)
  Hole size: 4mm(⁵⁄₃₂in)

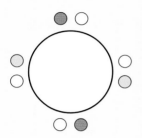

WARP DETAILS:

● 20 strands of light brown silk

○ 20 strands of tan silk

○ 20 strands of cream silk

WORKING

Whip both ends of the braid. Thread the bead on to one end and push it up out of the way (see Fig 39.2). Now butt the two ends together and sew them in place (see Fig 39.3). The first few stitches are always tricky and a small amount of glue can help to keep the braid ends in place. When the braid is secure, place a small amount of glue around the join and push the bead over it.

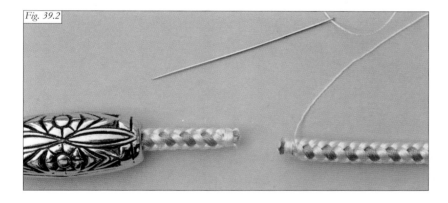

Fig. 39.2

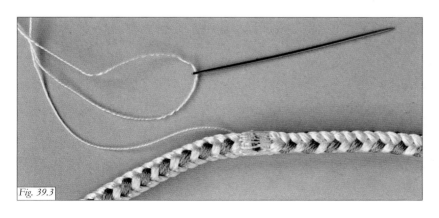

Fig. 39.3

Sample 39B

39. COVERED-SINGLE

SAMPLE 39C

BRAID DETAILS:

Braiding sequence: Square Braid

Bobbin weight: 70gms (2½oz)

Weight bag: 275gms (10oz)

BEAD DETAILS:

1 'Paper' bead made from a triangle of double thickness cream paper

Bead size: Base of triangle 3cm(1³⁄₁₆in)

Height of triangle 15cm(6in)

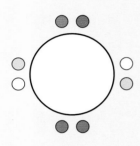

WARP DETAILS:

- 20 strands of light brown silk
- 20 strands of tan silk
- 20 strands of cream silk

WORKING

Here a paper bead is used to camouflage the join. Butt the two braid ends together and secure. Cut out a paper triangle with the dimensions given. Cover this with glue and roll it over the braid join.

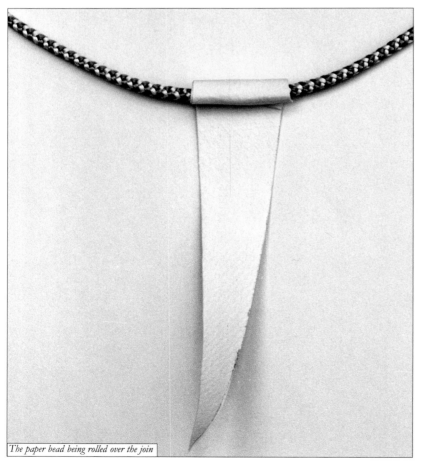

The paper bead being rolled over the join

Sample 39C

40 COVERED-MULTI

Here the two braid ends are joined in the same manner as shown on page 179. The join is then decorated with many beads.

SAMPLE 40A

BRAID DETAILS:

Braiding sequence: Flat Braid Two

Bobbin weight: 70gms (2½oz)

Weight bag: 275gms (10oz)

BEAD DETAILS:

40 red iridescent rocaille
  Bead size: 10/0

30 grey hexagonal rocaille
  Bead size: 11/0

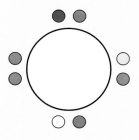

WARP DETAILS:

⬤ 20 strands of grey silk

⬤ 20 strands of pink silk

◯ 20 strands of pale pink silk

◯ 20 strands of cream silk

WORKING

Sew the two braid ends together as shown in Sample 39B. Bring the needle and thread out of the braid on one side of the join and add a series of seven alternate red and grey beads (see Fig 40.1) Take the thread into the braid on the other side of the join.

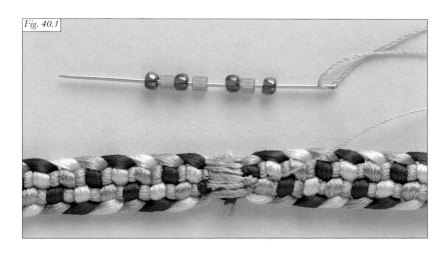

Fig. 40.1

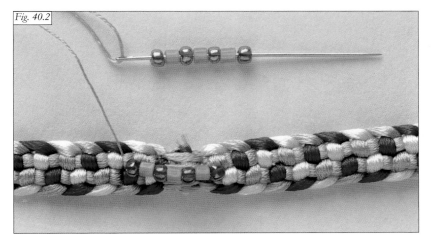

Fig. 40.2

Bring the needle out of the braid close to the end of the row of beads and add another series of seven beads (see Fig 40.2). Sew this row down parallel to the first row and continue round the join covering it with rows of beads.

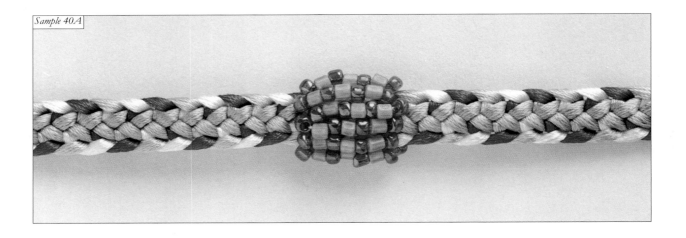

Sample 40A

SAMPLE 40B

BEAD DETAILS:

20 black bugle
    Bead size: 5mm(³⁄₁₆in)long
10 red iridescent rocaille
    Bead size: 10/0

BRAID DETAILS:

Braiding sequence: Flat Braid Two
Bobbin weight: 70gms (2½oz)
Weight bag: 275gms (10oz)

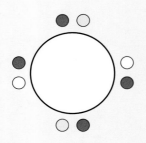

WARP DETAILS:

- ● 20 strands of pink silk
- ○ 20 strands of pale pink silk
- ○ 20 strands of cream silk

WORKING

Work in the same manner as
Sample 40A except add a series
of bugle, rocaille and bugle
beads on each row.

Sample 40B

SAMPLE 40C

BRAID DETAILS:

Braiding sequence: Flat Braid Two

Bobbin weight: 70gms (2½oz)

Weight bag: 275gms (10oz)

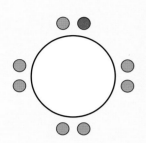

WARP DETAILS:

20 strands of grey silk

20 strands of pink silk

BEAD DETAILS:

20 red iridescent rocaille
    Bead size: 10/0
10 iridescent bugle
    Bead size: 7mm(⁵⁄₃₂in)long

WORKING

Work in the same manner as
Sample 40A except add a series
of rocaille, bugle and rocaille
beads on each row.

Sample 40C

GALLERY 34

An extravagant beaded tassel
on a large furnishing braid.